SALES &

OPERATIONS PLANNING

Also by Tom Wallace

Sales Forecasting – A New Approach

Master Scheduling in the 21st Century

ERP: Making It Happen

The Instant Access Guide to World Class Manufacturing

Customer Driven Strategy

The Innovation Edge

High Performance Purchasing

MRP II: Making It Happen

SALES &

OPERATIONS

PLANNING

The "How-To" Handbook

Second Edition

How to Implement It

How to Operate It

How to Use It to Benefit
Your Company, Your Customers,
and Your Supply Chain

Thomas F. Wallace

T. F. Wallace & Company
2004

Second Edition

First Printing: August 2004
Second Printing   November 2004, minor revisions

International Standard Book Number (ISBN): 0-9674884-4-3

Printed in the United States of America

Books may be ordered directly from the publisher:

T. F. Wallace & Company
453 Stanley Avenue
Cincinnati, Ohio 45226
(513) 281-0500
www.tfwallace.com

TABLE OF CONTENTS

Part One — What Is Sales & Operations Planning?

Part Two — How to Make It Work

List of Figures

Dedication

This book is dedicated to the men and women who work in America's manufacturing companies — in jobs that range from the plant floor to the executive suite, in roles that span the gamut from Sales & Marketing to Operations to Product Development to Finance & Accounting to Human Resources.

The manufacturing sector continues to be of paramount importance to the well-being of our country, economic and otherwise. The same can be said of the *people* who work in that sector, and thus our country owes you a large debt of gratitude.

Acknowledgments

Thanks also go to the talented and highly experienced professionals who reviewed the manuscripts of both the first and second editions of this book and gave invaluable feedback.

First Edition:

Ross Bushman
Vice President, Sales and Planning
Cast-Fab Technologies

Mike Kremzar
former Vice President, Product Supply
The Procter & Gamble Company

Dick Ling
President
Richard C. Ling, Inc.

Arvil Sexton
former Vice President, Mfg. Resource Planning
Drexel Heritage Furnishings, Inc.

Chandler Stevens
Production Planning
CTL Aerospace

Mike Campbell
President and CEO
Demand Management, Inc.

Linda LeBlanc
Vice President, Human Resources
Formica Corporation

Walt Pietrak
North American MRP II Coach
The Procter & Gamble Company

Bing Sherrill
Vice President, General Manager
Moog, Inc. Systems Group

Second Edition:

Chris Gray
President
Gray Research

Rebecca Morgan
Principal
The Fulcrum Consulting Works

Bob Stahl
President
R. A. Stahl Company

Bill Montgomery
Orange County CA APICS Chapter

Arvil Sexton
former Vice President, Mfg. Resource Planning
Drexel Heritage Furnishings, Inc.

Thanks, folks, you made the book a lot better.

In addition to once again providing superb feedback as a reviewer, Chris Gray wrote Appendix A, which addresses the linkage between S&OP and Lean Manufacturing. Chris is an expert in both topics, and we're fortunate to benefit from his expertise in this book. Thanks, Chris.

Many thanks also go to Kathryn Wallace (page layout), Kim Nir (copy edit), and David Mill (cover design). These folks did their usual superb job, for which we're very grateful.

Another special acknowledgment goes to my friend and colleague, Arvil Sexton. Arvil's enthusiasm, dedication, and commitment to helping improve American industry mark him as one of the true professionals in this field. Without him, the first edition of this book probably wouldn't have been written. Thanks, Arvil.

Ditto for Bob Stahl, also a real professional and also a good friend. Bob's support and "gentle encouragement" played a large part in the creation of this second edition. For that and for so much else, thank you, sir.

Foreword

Sales & Operations Planning (S&OP) is a superior decision-making process that helps people in companies to provide excellent customer service and to run the business better. It's a great tool, when it's done correctly. However, in my travels, I see too many companies:

- trying to use S&OP but struggling, because they really don't understand it; or,

- trying to implement S&OP but having a hard time, because they really don't understand it; or,

- not considering S&OP, because they really don't understand it.

There's a fair amount of misinformation and mythology about Sales & Operations Planning that's getting in the way. For example ...

Myth: S&OP's just a once-per-month meeting.

Fact: S&OP operates on a monthly cycle, which culminates in the Executive S&OP meeting held around the middle of the month. Prior to that, three important phases take place: Demand Planning, Supply Planning, and the Pre-SOP meeting, where middle management people formulate recommendations for the executive session.

All of these activities make it possible for the Executive S&OP meeting to take place in two hours or less, thereby making very effective use of top management's time. Sales & Operations Planning is an ongoing, multistep process that occurs every month.

****

Myth: S&OP's no big deal — it's mainly looking at numbers on a spreadsheet.

Fact: The essence of S&OP is decision-making regarding customer service goals, sales volumes, production rates, levels of finished goods or intermediate inventory, and customer order backlog. The S&OP spreadsheet, one for each major product family, brings all of these elements together into one display.

S&OP enables people to view the business holistically — to see the interplay between demand and supply, between customer orders and inventories — and to make solid, informed decisions. Viewing different parts of the business separately can lead people to make suboptimal decisions, as in "the inventories are too high, cut the inventory!" and "our customer service is lousy; we've got to put more into inventories!" An organic, holistic view of the business makes it far easier to avoid such decisions — and to avoid getting into that kind of trouble in the first place.

****

Myth: S&OP deals with product families, so how can it be helpful? You can't learn anything from looking at aggregate numbers.

Fact: We do it all the time. Take investing, for example. When I want to know how the stock market's doing, I check the Dow Jones Industrial Average, the S&P 500, and the Nasdaq. Those three numbers alone give me a good feel for what the market's doing. If they haven't changed a lot from yesterday, last week, last month, then I'm okay and can think about something else. If there's a lot of movement, however, then I may want to get down into the detail and check my individual mutual funds and stocks.

It's similar for a manufacturing enterprise. The picture on aggregate product families shows:

  • their levels of customer service;

  • how their sales are trending;

  • whether production is meeting the overall plan; and

  • whether the finished inventories and customer order backlogs are where we want them to be, and so on.

With this high-level information, executives and managers can make effective decisions regarding the direction of these important elements of the business. I liken this view of the business to flying in a plane at about 5000 feet off the ground. You can see a lot from up there; you can get the big picture.

Of course, the company has to do more than deal with aggregate volumes. It needs to handle the mix — individual products, customer orders, stockkeeping units. This is the job of tools such as line-item forecasting, customer order promising, master scheduling, and plant and supplier scheduling. Mix is not the big picture; it's the details. Mix is 200 feet off the ground at about 400 knots. I can guarantee you that you can't see the big picture down there.

****

Myth: Sales & Operations Planning is just a new term for something that's been around forever — Production Planning.

Fact: The difference between Production Planning and Sales & Operations Planning is as large as the differences between functional silos and cross-functional teams. The old Production Planning process — the "silo" approach — called for Sales and Marketing to develop the sales forecast and hand it off to Operations for production planning. The resulting production plan was then given to the Master Scheduler to break down into individual products. That's it.

Sales & Operations Planning — a cross-functional process — calls for Sales and Marketing, Operations, Finance, and Product Development to work together to develop an integrated set of plans that all of these departments can support. Then their recommendations are presented to the Executive S&OP Team (another cross-functional group) for their approval or decisions to modify the recommendations. The output of this process is the authorized company-wide game plan, far more than a production plan. For more on this topic, see Appendix D.

****

I wrote this book to dispel the myths and to raise awareness of the facts. My hope is that it will help more and more companies take advantage of the powerful decision-making capabilities of S&OP, which in turn will help them to run their businesses better.

Tom Wallace
Cincinnati, Ohio and Bryson City, North Carolina
June 1999

Foreword to the Second Edition

Much can happen in five years — the span of time between the first edition of this book until now. This edition is intended to address topics that the first book covered only partially or not at all.

Much of the material in the first edition remains, and that's gratifying. The body of knowledge making up Sales & Operations Planning (S&OP) remains much the same; it's evolving but not changing dramatically. What's been added to this new edition, mainly, is how S&OP is used in a variety of different environments:

Lean Manufacturing

Global Businesses

Highly Seasonal Products

Finish-to-Order/Build-to-Order /Postponement

Supply Chain Management

In addition, you'll find new material on Graphical S&OP displays, Rough-Cut Capacity Planning, education for S&OP, and fixing a broken S&OP process. I do hope it's helpful.

Tom Wallace
Cincinnati, Ohio and Bryson City, North Carolina
June 2004

How to Use This Book

This book has two major sections. Part One introduces and describes Sales & Operations Planning, while Part Two, the larger section, focuses on how to make it work.

Time is money, and typically we don't have enough of either. Not everybody will need to — much less want to — read all of this book. So here are some thoughts as to who might read which chapters, in order to learn what they need to know and still make efficient use of their time.

Companies Operating S&OP

A number of companies today are using Sales & Operations Planning to help manage their businesses, some very successfully. If you're in that category, you probably know quite a bit about S&OP already. Therefore, Part One of this book, which describes the process, may not add much value for you. However, Part Two, which gets into the details of how to implement it, might help you make improvements. My advice for you folks is to read Chapters 6 through 17 (that's all of Part Two) and double back into Part One if you feel the need for clarification.

Many people I talk to in companies using Sales & Operations Planning are curious about how they're doing and how they stack up against other S&OP users. If you're in that category, you might first look at the S&OP Effectiveness Checklist in Chapter 16. It should give you a good idea concerning the strong and the not-so-strong aspects of your process and help you prioritize the needed changes.

Companies Implementing S&OP

People in these companies fall into several categories (described in Chapter 7):

- Members of the Executive S&OP Team should read at least Chapters 1 through 7.

- The Executive Champion and the S&OP Process Owner should read the entire book.

- Anyone who will be "hands-on" with Sales & Operations Planning should read the entire book, including members of the Pre-SOP Team, Demand Planning Team, and Supply Planning Team.

- The senior Information Systems executive should read Chapters 9 and 14, in addition to Chapters 1 through 7.

- The Spreadsheet Developer should read Chapters 1 through 9.

Companies Considering S&OP

This book can also be helpful to people in companies that have not yet begun an implementation. Typically they want to know what it is, how it works, why it's important, and how it might help them. They should read Chapters 1 through 5. Then, if that gets their interest, they might want to cover the remaining chapters.

Part One

What Is Sales & Operations Planning?

Chapter 1

Sales & Operations Planning Overview

Let's eavesdrop on an executive staff meeting at the Acme Widget Company. The participants are not happy campers.

President: *This shortage situation is terrible. When will we ever get our act together? Whenever business gets good, we run out of product and our customer service is lousy.*

VP Operations: *I'll tell you when. When we start to get some decent forecasts from the Sales Department ...*

VP Sales (interrupting): *Wait a minute. We forecasted this upturn.*

VP Operations: *... in time to do something about it. Yeah, we got the revised forecast — four days after the start of the month. By then it was too late.*

VP Sales: *I could have told you months ago. All you had to do was ask.*

VP Finance: *I'd like to be in on those conversations. We've been burned more than once by building inventories for a business upturn that doesn't happen. Then we get stuck with tons of inventory and run out of cash.*

And the beat goes on: back orders, dissatisfied customers, high inventories, late shipments, finger pointing, cash-flow problems, demand and supply out of balance, missing the business plan. This is the norm in many companies.

It does not, however, have to be that way. Today many companies are using a business process called Sales & Operations Planning (S&OP) to help avoid such problems. To learn what it is, and how to make it work, read on.

What Is Sales & Operations Planning?

How would you like to have a process that has helped many companies give better customer service, lower your inventories, shorten customer lead times, stabilize production rates, work better with suppliers, give top management a real handle on the business, and build teamwork between Sales, Operations, Finance, and Product Development? How much would that be worth to you?

Such a process exists. Would you like this tool to be relatively easy to implement, not cost much, and start to generate results within a few months of getting started? It's all of those things. It's called Sales & Operations Planning (S&OP), and a growing number of companies are using it to sharply improve their ability to run their businesses. It helps them to get demand and supply in balance, *and to keep them in balance.* Balancing demand and supply is essential to running a business well, and this balancing must occur at both the aggregate, volume level and at the detailed, mix level.

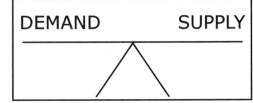

We've just identified four fundamentals: demand and supply, volume and mix. Let's look at the first pair.

Demand and Supply

What happens when demand and supply aren't in balance? Well, if demand greatly exceeds supply, bad things happen:

- Customer service suffers. The company can't ship product to its customers when they want it. Customer lead times stretch out as the order backlog builds. Business is lost as customers go elsewhere.

- Costs increase. Unplanned overtime goes up. Material costs may increase. Premium freight rises.

- Quality often "gets lost in the shuffle" as the company strives mightily to get product shipped. Specifications get compromised or waived. Temporary subcontracting yields a less robust product. Material from alternate suppliers often doesn't process as well.

Isn't this great? Owing to demand exceeding supply, performance can deteriorate on three fundamental attributes: cost, quality, and delivery. Business is lost, costs go up, and thus the bottom line takes a hit. Similarly, when supply substantially exceeds demand, bad things happen:

- Inventories increase, carrying costs rise, and cash flow can become a problem.

- Production rates are cut. Volume variances turn unfavorable. Layoffs are a possibility and morale suffers. People in the plant slow down and efficiency numbers start to drop.

- Profit margins get squeezed. Prices are cut. Discounting increases. Deals and promotions become more frequent.

Well, that's not good either. Supply exceeds demand and the company is stuck with lower margins, higher costs, a cash crunch, and the possibility of layoffs.

Now, is it always bad if demand and supply aren't in balance? No, sometimes it can be a good thing. It all depends on where the imbalance lies. For example, if projected demand ten months in the future exceeds current supply, and if the company can economically add more capacity sooner than that, that's fine. Demand is growing; business is good. Being able to see the projected imbalances soon enough is what's needed, so that the *potential* imbalance problems can be eliminated before they become real problems.

At the risk of stating the obvious, I'd like to point out that demand and supply are not the same thing. Demand is what the customers — external and internal — want; supply represents the resources we have available to meet that demand. We all know that, so why am I taking up your time with it?

Well, I sometimes see companies struggling with demand/supply issues, but not being very effective. They're often unable to answer the fundamental question: Is this a demand problem or is it a supply problem? The result is a lack of focus, which can lead a less than desirable outcome. Rather, in our thinking, we should *decouple demand from supply*. Study and analyze them *separately*, so that they can be brought together *in the real world*.

The next time you're in a discussion about bad customer service, excessive inventories, erratic plant schedules, or the like, ask yourselves: Is this primarily a demand problem or a supply problem? Get agreement among your colleagues on that point, and often you'll be well on the way to solving the problem.

The name of the game therefore is to get demand and supply *in balance* and to keep them there. It's that simple. Balance demand and supply. Have processes in place to do it. Have early warning capabilities to alert people that they're getting out of sync. Make the necessary corrections early — surgically — so that they can be small, as opposed to making large, radical corrections later with a meat cleaver.

Volume and Mix

The other two fundamentals are volume and mix. As with demand and supply, we need to treat them separately in our thinking. If volume is handled effectively, it's much less difficult to deal with mix problems as they arise. On the other hand, if volume is not planned well, then mix issues become substantially more difficult to cope with. Many companies get themselves in trouble because they can't distinguish volume-related problems from those of mix. In the box below, we can see the difference between the two: volume is the big picture and mix is the details.

Questions of volume precede those of mix, so smart companies plan their volumes first, and spend enough time and effort to do it well. They find that doing so makes mix problems easier to deal with. But where do most companies spend almost all of their time? On mix. Many look at volumes only once per year, when they do the Business Plan. They probably wouldn't do it even that often, except that the folks in Finance & Accounting make them do it. Once each year, the CFO says, "Well, folks, it's budget time again."

```
┌─────────────────────────────────────────────┐
│            Volume versus Mix                  │
│                                               │
│  Volume    =    The Big Picture:              │
│                     How Much?                 │
│                     Rates                     │
│                     Product Families          │
│                                               │
│  Mix       =    The Details:                  │
│                     Which Ones?               │
│                     Sequence                  │
│                     Individual Products and   │
│                     Customer Orders           │
└─────────────────────────────────────────────┘
```

Why is that? Why do most companies spend more than 99 percent of their time on mix issues to the exclusion of volume? It's simple: mix — individual products — is what companies ship to their customers. That's where the pressure is. Mix is seen as important and urgent. The effective planning of future volumes may be seen as important, but it carries less urgency.

As a result, many companies set their volumes — sales rates and production rates — no more than once per year, when they do their annual business plan. But how often during an average year do volume needs change? It's almost always more often than once every twelve months. For most companies, it's more than once per quarter.

I submit that most companies don't work hard enough at forecasting and planning their volumes and *spend too much time trying to predict mix*. They overwork the details and don't focus enough on the big picture.

Back to the four fundamentals: demand and supply, volume and mix. Shipping product to customers with world-class reliability and speed requires that all four of these elements be well managed and controlled.

S&OP's mission is to balance demand and supply at the *volume* level. Volume refers to rates — overall rates of sales, rates of production, aggregate inventories, and order backlogs. Companies have found that when they do a good job of planning and replanning volume (rates and levels) as they go through the year, then problems with *mix* (individual products and orders) become less difficult to deal with. Companies have found they can ship better and more quickly, and do it with less inventory.

For those of you who like formal definitions, I offer this:

> Sales & Operations Planning (S&OP) is a business process that helps companies keep **demand and supply in balance.** It does that by focusing on **aggregate volumes** (product families and groups) so that mix issues (individual products and customer orders) can be handled more readily. It occurs on a **monthly** cycle and displays information in both **units and dollars,** thus it integrates operational and financial planning. S&OP is **crossfunctional,** involving General Management, Sales, Operations, Finance, and Product Development. It occurs at **multiple levels** within the company, up to and **including the executive in charge of the business unit,** e.g., division president, business unit general manager, or CEO of a smaller corporation. S&OP **links the company's Strategic Plans and Business Plan to its detailed processes** — the order entry, master scheduling, plant scheduling, and purchasing tools it uses to run the business on a week-to-week, day-to-day, and hour-to-hour basis. Used properly, S&OP enables the company's managers to view the business **holistically** and gives them a **window into the future.**

What Are the Benefits?

Benefits resulting from effective Sales & Operations Planning include:

• For Make-to-Stock companies: higher customer service and often lower finished goods inventories — *at the same time.*

• For Make-to-Order companies: higher customer service, and often smaller customer order backlogs and hence shorter lead times — *at the same time.*

• For Finish-to-Order/postponement companies[1]: higher customer service, quicker response, and often lower component inventories — *at the same time.*

• More stable production rates and less overtime, leading to higher productivity.

• Better visibility into future capacity problems, both too much work and too little.

---

[1] The Finish-to-Order strategy means to postpone finishing the product until the customer order is received and then finishing it very quickly out of available components. Dell Computer is the best known example of this. More on this later.

• Enhanced teamwork among the middle-management people from Sales, Operations, Finance, and Product Development.[2]

• Enhanced teamwork within the executive group.

• Greater accountability regarding actual performance to plan.

• A better demand/supply balance across the company's supply chain.

• A monthly update to the Business Plan, leading to better forward visibility and fewer surprises late in the fiscal year.

• The establishment of "one set of numbers" with which to run the business.[3] The primary functional areas of the business — Sales/Marketing, Operations, Finance, Product Development, and General Management — all operate with a common game plan.

• The ability to make changes *quickly* off of that common game plan.

• A sharp decrease in the amount of *detailed* forecasting and scheduling required, because the volume plans in S&OP eliminate the need for detailed mix plans extending far into the future.[4]

• Last and certainly not least, S&OP provides as we said a "window into the future." It's uncanny, but the process — when done well — truly does enable people to better see future problems coming at them: a large increase in workload several months out, an upcoming new product launch that will consume substantial plant capacity, a forecasted downturn in demand later in the year. S&OP enhances proactive decision-making.

My colleague, Chris Gray, makes a good point about communications as a benefit: "People complain that 'our company doesn't communicate well' and this becomes the diagnosis for all the ills in the company. Of course by saying that, they don't mean that the solution is better voice mail or e-mail or another technology approach. They know that they need better processes to *istitutionalize* communications, so that Charlie doesn't have to remember to tell Fred about the slip in the new

---

[2] Throughout this book, I use the term "Sales" to refer to all of the sales and marketing functions throughout the company, i.e., the demand side of the business. "Operations" refers to the manufacturing, supply chain, materials, and logistics functions, i.e., the supply-side activities.

[3] Some publicly traded companies operate on the principle of: "under-promise and over-deliver." They'll use two sets of numbers: one for Wall Street, containing plans expected to be attained, and one for internal purposes with stretch goals, which may or may not be completely achieved. That's fine. They run with one set of *internal* numbers – the stretch goals – and that's what we're talking about here.

[4] For more on this, see Wallace, Thomas F. and Stahl, Robert A., *Master Scheduling in the 21st Century*, Cincinnati, OH, T.F. Wallace & Company, 2003, pp 47– 52

product roll out and so that Betty doesn't have to remember to communicate with Finance about a potential problem in hitting the estimates for the year, etc. For me, S&OP is as much about *institutionalizing communications* throughout the organization as it is anything else."

Executives who've implemented S&OP swear by it. Let's hear from some:

- *Sales & Operations Planning addresses the very same issues that are vital to our customers — what they need and how we're going to get it to them.* — Vice President, Sales

- *Because we're looking ahead every month, we're able to make production rate changes sooner and, at times, spread the impact. This means these changes are easier for us and our work force to respond to. And they cost less.* — Vice President, Operations

- *The benefits from Sales & Operations Planning have been significant and continue to grow. Some of our business units have experienced a 20 percent improvement in customer service levels while costs have decreased.* — Vice President, Product Supply

- *In some of our Make-to-Order businesses, as a direct result of S&OP we've reduced lead times to customers by up to 50 percent.* — Vice President/Group General Manager

Perhaps the best testimonial of all came from the head of the North American component of a UK-based multinational. At the conclusion of an S&OP meeting where some very difficult decisions were made, he turned to me and said:

Tom, when I think back to a year ago, before we had S&OP, I wonder how we were able to run the business without it. — Division Chief Executive

Sales & Operations Planning really is top management's handle on the business.

Why Is Top Management Necessary?

Saying it another way, does the boss really need to be involved, and if so, why? Well, I believe that active, involved leadership and participation by the head of the business unit is essential for S&OP to work anywhere near its full potential. The two main reasons are stewardship and leadership:

- Many of the decisions made in S&OP affect the Financial Plan for the current year, and top management "owns" that Business Plan. They have a *stewardship* responsibility for it, because they represent the shareholders, partners, family, etc. Thus, only they can make decisions to change it. When the Business Plan is not changed to reflect the new Sales & Operations Plan, there's a disconnect between the financial numbers top management is expecting and the sales forecasts and operations plans being used to operate the business. "Best in class" performance in this area means that the business is managed using only one set of internal numbers.

- Participation by the *heads* of the business makes a strong *leadership* statement that S&OP is the process being used to manage these important activities: integrating operational and financial planning, balancing demand and supply, and enhancing customer service. This "encourages" people throughout the organization to do their part. Without such leadership by top management, participation in the S&OP process can be viewed as optional, with the result that over time, the process erodes and goes away, or deteriorates into a high-level shortage meeting.

Participation by the executive group shouldn't be a problem, because so relatively little of their time is required. We're talking about one meeting per month, lasting for two hours or less. This event, called the Executive Sales & Operations Planning meeting, can often replace several other meetings and thus result in a net reduction in meeting time. For presidents, preparation time is zero. For members of the president's staff, some preparation time may be helpful — mainly in the form of briefings by their people — to enable the necessary sign-offs to take place.

So how can something so productive require so little time? Well, most of the heavy lifting is done in earlier steps: middle-management people update the forecast and demand plan, identify capacity issues and raw material problems, and formulate recommendations for the Executive S&OP meeting.

How Does S&OP Connect the Pieces?

In companies without S&OP, there is frequently a disconnect between the Strategic and Business (financial) Plans and the detailed plans and schedules. In other words, the plans developed and authorized by top management are not connected to the plans and schedules that drive day-to-day activities on the plant floor, the receiving dock, and most important, the shipping dock.

The vice president/general manager of a two billion dollar per year consumer goods business had an interesting way of putting it. He said, "Before we had S&OP in the company, I spent a lot of my time turning knobs that weren't connected to anything." What he was saying is that the decisions he made at his level may or may not have gotten transmitted down to impact directly what happened on the

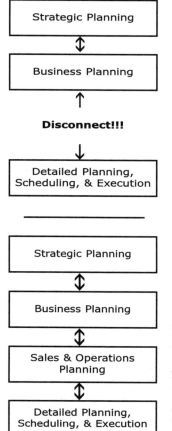

plant floor, the receiving dock, and perhaps most important of all, in the customer order department and on the shipping dock. Or, if they did get communicated, they might get garbled on the way down. Or two or more other things might get messed up in the process. There was a disconnect in the process.

He went on to say, "S&OP connects the knobs." S&OP links the top-level strategic and financial plans of the business to the week-to-week, day-to-day, or shift-to-shift activities of receiving and promising customer orders, acquiring material, converting it into finished product, and shipping it to customers.

How Much Does S&OP Cost?

Surprisingly little. It involves relatively few people: dozens, not hundreds, in an average-sized business of, say, $100 to $500 million. Thus, the education and training costs are low. It normally doesn't require a full-time project team or even, frequently, a full-time project leader. Software plays a relatively minor role in Sales & Operations Planning, so computer costs range from moderate to zero.

Regarding the latter point, many companies have found that S&OP will require that they do a better job of forecasting and that good forecasting software will help them do that. Some companies already have all they need; the most popular spreadsheet software package has surprisingly good support for forecasting.[5] For the S&OP spreadsheet itself, most companies also use a spreadsheet package. More on software later; for now, just be aware that it shouldn't cost you very much at all.

The other expenditure that some companies incur is consulting costs. We'll discuss this aspect of implementation in Chapter 8, but for now let's just point out that these costs are typically around $50,000 over the life of the six- to ten-month implementation cycle.

To sum up, if you decide to buy forecasting and S&OP software and to use a consultant, the project will cost under $100,000 for an average business unit. If you don't need software and are able to use an experienced internal advisor, your out-of-pocket costs will be near zero.

---

[5] This is good enough to get started but may not provide enough capabilities over the long run. Happily, there are software offerings that can be added on to the basic spreadsheet that give most companies all the tools they'll ever need.

Some experienced S&OP users claim that the benefits from Sales & Operations Planning equal or exceed those from their ERP initiative. S&OP typically costs less than $100,000; installing an ERP software system often costs millions of dollars.

FREQUENTLY ASKED QUESTIONS

Sales & Operations Planning sounds pretty formal. Is it too rigid?

Dick Ling, the "inventor" of the process, says it very well: "S&OP's all about managing change." Think about it: if things never changed, or changed only once per year, there would be no need for S&OP. It's there because things change.

Sales & Operations Planning gives you the ability to make changes very quickly because there's an agreed-upon game plan already in place. Without S&OP, there's seldom a total plan; each department has its own. With S&OP, the foundation's already there because the key players have already bought into one single plan. All that needs to be addressed are the deltas arising from new conditions.

S&OP is far from rigid. It's a tool to manage change.

Chapter 2

Where Does S&OP Fit?

In this chapter, we'll focus on how S&OP relates to three well-known initiatives: Enterprise Resource Planning, Supply Chain Management, and last but certainly not least, Lean Manufacturing.

How Does S&OP Interact with Enterprise Resource Planning?

First, a point of clarification: Enterprise Resource Planning (ERP) is not a set of software. That may surprise some of you, since the business press and some consulting firms have twisted this around a good bit. ERP is a set of *business functions* for resource planning. A set of software that supports ERP is properly called an Enterprise Software System (ESS).[1]

The predecessor to ERP was Manufacturing Resource Planning (MRP II). The differences between it and ERP are not great. One way to think of ERP is that it's essentially MRPII running on an Enterprise Software System (ESS). In that context, ERP/ES is more robust and is better able to integrate operations within diverse business units. At the heart of all of this are the *business processes* to balance demand and supply, provide superior customer service, and manage the resources of the business well.

S&OP was originally developed as a part of the resource planning process. It started out as *Production Planning* and then, thanks to pioneering work by Dick Ling, developed into Sales & Operations Planning. (For a comparison of S&OP with Production Planning, please see Appendix E.)

At this point, it may be helpful to look at Figure 2-1, which depicts the structure of the resource planning process. The horizontal dotted line indicates that Strategic Planning and Business Planning are not integral parts of the overall resource planning process. Rather, they are important drivers into the process.

Sales & Operations Planning, as we saw earlier, forms an essential linkage. It ties the Strategic and Business Plans together with the Master Scheduling function. It's the Master Schedule that serves as the source of customer order promising and drives all of the "downstream" schedules for the plants and the suppliers.

---

[1] For more on this distinction, please see Thomas H. Davenport, *Mission Critical – Realizing the Promise of Enterprise Systems* (Boston: Harvard Business School Press, 2000) and Thomas F. Wallace and Michael H. Kremzar, *ERP: Making It Happen – The Implementers' Guide to Success with Enterprise Resource Planning* (New York: John Wiley & Sons, 2001).

Figure 2-1

THE RESOURCE PLANNING MODEL
(Manufacturing Resource Planning, Business Resource Planning, Enterprise Resource Planning)

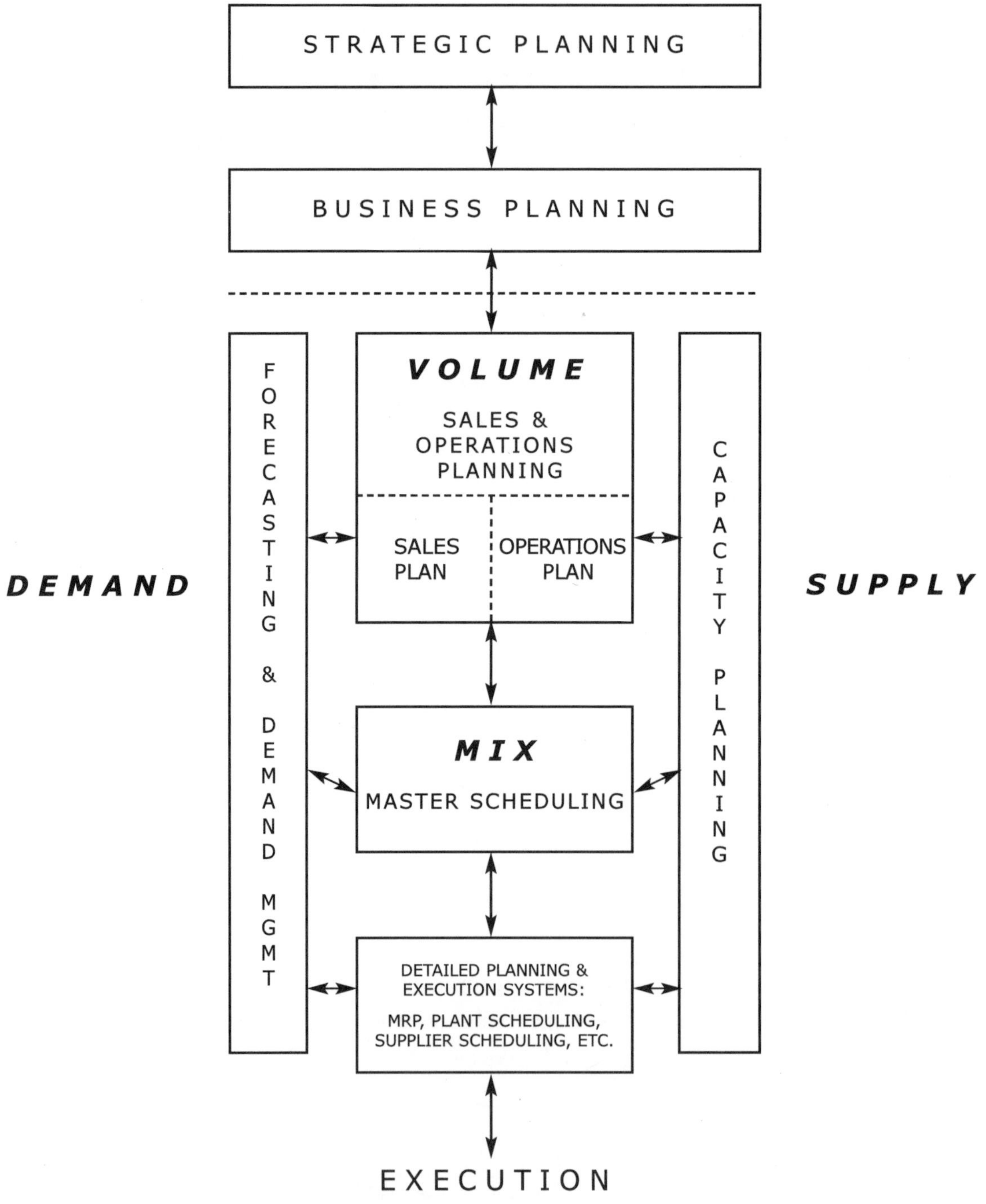

STRATEGIC PLANNING

BUSINESS PLANNING

DEMAND

FORECASTING & DEMAND MGMT

VOLUME

SALES & OPERATIONS PLANNING

| SALES PLAN | OPERATIONS PLAN |

MIX

MASTER SCHEDULING

DETAILED PLANNING & EXECUTION SYSTEMS:

MRP, PLANT SCHEDULING, SUPPLIER SCHEDULING, ETC.

CAPACITY PLANNING

SUPPLY

EXECUTION

How Does S&OP Support Supply Chain Management?

S&OP does more than support Supply Chain Management; it's an integral part of it. A given supply chain probably won't work well if its various members don't have good volume plans in the first place and if they're slow to react to the inevitable changes in volume. Sales & Operations Planning can be considered as a *lubricant* between partners in the supply chain, enabling the total chain to function harmoniously and with minimum disruption.

Supply chains extend in two directions: forward to the customers and backward to suppliers, with the company itself at the center of that chain (see Figure 2-2). If that company, the one at the center of the chain, doesn't do a good job of balancing its own demand and supply, then what are the chances that its supply chain partners will receive valid statements of future demand and supply to produce against? Two chances: slim and none.

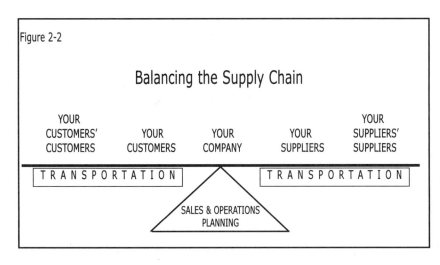

Figure 2-2

Balancing the Supply Chain

Regarding customer service, we've already seen examples and heard testimonials from executives on S&OP's contribution to improved customer service perform-ance. And for me this is the biggest supply chain benefit of all: *S&OP will help you provide superior customer service.*

Regarding moving backward in the supply chain, toward the suppliers, S&OP's contribution is also significant. The benefits can be much the same for suppliers as for a company's internal production processes. Provided the company shares some of its S&OP results with key suppliers, then these suppliers should experience:

• more stable production rates,

• volume changes made sooner and smaller, and hence more economically — rather than later and larger, and thus more expensively,

• a greater ability to respond to mix changes, because volume is under control.

Supplier partnering calls for shared information and plans. This is based on the premise that the more advance notice you can give suppliers, the better they will be able to support your needs. Very simply, S&OP can help to provide the future volume plans for suppliers — off the same common plan that top management has authorized for internal production.

Procter & Gamble does a superb job of managing its supply chains. Mike Kremzar, who served as Vice President, Product Supply Worldwide during that company's drive to supply chain excellence, sums it up: "With an effective S&OP process, the supply chain can be optimized to become a true competitive advantage with costs, speed, and inventories at levels thought to be unreachable."

How Does S&OP Support Lean Manufacturing?

S&OP supports Lean Manufacturing in much the same way that it supports a conventional manufacturing environment:

- It involves decision-making on future rates of demand and supply.

- It operates at an aggregate level and ties the aggregate to the detail.

- It integrates financial plans and operational plans.

- It involves top management in decision-making on these issues.

- It provides a window into the future.

To understand more deeply how Lean Manufacturing and S&OP work together, let's look at the differences between Lean and ERP. They're not the same thing at all. Lean is an approach, a methodology, a mind-set focusing intensely on the elimination of waste. It's centered largely, but notexclusively, on physical processes. Its mission is to improve the operating environment.

Lean Manufacturing	Resource Planning
• Tools to reduce waste, cost, and time • Strong on execution • Short future horizon • Drives improvements to the operating environment • Works best with stable and linear demand	• Tools for forward decision-making • Strong on planning • Long future horizon • Balances demand and supply across the supply chain • Can be used in many different environments

ERP, on the other hand, is primarily a set of planning tools. It accepts the environment that has been described to it; it will help you to maximize performance out of the environment you've described to it.

Many successful users of Lean Manufacturing also use parts of ERP. Let's look back to Figure 2-1 and ask ourselves a few questions:

- Do Lean companies need to do strategic and business (financial) planning? Yes.

- Do they need to forecast and manage customer demand? Yes, frequently only in aggregate, not at the individual item level.

- Do they need to plan future capacities? Yes, but they may do it differently from the standard method in ERP, called Rough-Cut Capacity Planning.

- Do they need to Master Schedule? Yes, and in Lean shops it's sometimes referred to as the Master Schedule and in other cases as the *Pacemaker Schedule.*[2]

- Do they need to do the things in the bottom box on page 14: Material Requirements Planning (MRP), Plant Scheduling, Supplier Scheduling? This is the area of greatest difference. Plant Scheduling in Lean happens very differently from the traditional shop floor control portion of ERP. (It's much simpler in Lean, because the plant environment has been made simpler.)

Supplier Scheduling, derived from MRP, is frequently used for medium- to long-range planning, while the primary scheduling tool is frequently a Kanban-based demand pull approach[3] made possible by flow and level schedules within Lean.

So, in terms of strategic and financial planning, aggregate forecasting, demand management, and master scheduling, there are far more similarities than differences. In companies using both S&OP and Lean Manufacturing, S&OP operates much as it does in a traditional environment, with perhaps some enhancements to the S&OP spreadsheet format, an example of which is shown in Appendix A.

---

[2] For more on this, see Thomas F. Wallace and Robert A. Stahl, *Master Scheduling in the 21st Century*, (Cincinnati, T.F. Wallace & Company, 2003, Appendix F).

[3] Kanban is a visual scheduling technique that signals the need for replenishment.

Further, many people in companies who make effective use of Lean Manufacturing and of the "upper elements" within ERP (S&OP, Demand Management, and Master Scheduling) will tell you: *they work best when they work together. You need 'em both.*

Perhaps the major difference in how S&OP is used in a Lean environment is that the rates set in S&OP can form the basis for calculating values such as *Takt Time, Operational Takt Time,* and *Engineered Cycle Time.* These are important to Lean but play a lesser role, or none, in a plant operating conventionally. We'll look more closely at these elements in Chapter 4.

FREQUENTLY ASKED QUESTIONS

We don't have a full-blown resource planning system (ERP/MRP II) in our company. Does that mean we can't use Sales & Operations Planning?

Not at all. Even though S&OP was developed as an integral part of MRP II/ERP, it's been proven to work very well on a stand-alone basis or, as we just saw, in a Lean Manufacturing environment that uses only parts of ERP. My advice: don't delay S&OP waiting for the implementation of a full-blown resource planning system. Get started now so you can start to get the benefits from S&OP. Then, if and when you do implement a resource planning system, it'll work much better because you'll have demand and supply balanced at the volume level.

Keep in mind that most ERP software systems deal almost entirely with issues of *mix,* not volume. One reason so many companies have been bitterly disappointed with the results from their massive investments in software for ERP is, quite simply, they haven't implemented S&OP. Why not? Frequently it's because no S&OP module came with their ERP software package. Thus, it's not on the radar screen of the project team and system integrators. Therefore, it doesn't get done.

The result is that the company is left with software, and sometimes better processes, to help manage the mix — but *volume* is being addressed formally only once per year. So if this scenario describes your company, consider that S&OP could give you the opportunity to make sure your ERP investment really pays off.

Chapter 3

The Structure and Logic of Sales & Operations Planning

What follows is an example from a fictitious manufacturer of widgets for home and industry. This company is not yet using Sales & Operations Planning.

Bad Day at Acme Widget

Mike Marshall, a product manager at Acme Widget, is doing his quarterly review of the forecasts for his products. He's looking at a summary spreadsheet for the Medium Consumer Widget product family.

	FEB	MAR	APR	MAY	JUN	JUL	AUG	SEP
FORECAST (in 000 units)	100	100	100	100	120	120	120	120
ACTUAL SALES	90	95	85					
DIFFERENCE	−10	−5	−15					
CUM DIFFERENCE		−15	−30					

Mike is concerned that sales are consistently below forecast. Over the last three months, actual sales have been 10 percent less than forecast. Mike scratches his head, checks a couple of reports he recently received from field sales people, and concludes that this product family is losing business to another family that the company introduced recently. He decides to revise the forecast downward and, with a few quick strokes on his computer keyboard, does so.

	FEB	MAR	APR		MAY	JUN	JUL	AUG	SEP
FORECAST (in 000 units)	100	100	100	OLD FORECAST	100	120	120	120	120
				NEW FORECAST	90	90	90	90	90
ACTUAL SALES	90	95	85						
DIFFERENCE	−10	−5	−15						
CUM DIFFERENCE		−15	−30						

Mike has reduced his forecast by 10,000 per month in May and by 30,000 per month after that, thereby wiping out the forecast increase that he had made for June and beyond. Remembering a conversation he had recently with Carol Clark, the chief financial officer, about high inventories, he decides to notify the plant of the forecast change. He sends Pete Prentis, the plant manager, an e-mail, containing the spreadsheet shown above.

Pete reacts to the e-mail message by checking his production plan for Medium Consumer Widgets:

	FEB	MAR	APR	MAY	JUN	JUL	AUG	SEP
PLANNED PRODUCTION (in 000 units)	100	100	100	110	120	120	120	120
ACTUAL PRODUCTION	98	100	101					
DIFFERENCE	−2	—	+1					
CUM DIFFERENCE	−2	−2	−1					

Pete scratches his head and thinks to himself, *Man, this is a double whammy. Not only is he dropping the forecast, he's taking out the increase set for June. And we're already ramping up to 120,000 per month. Nuts!* Pete calls Mike; they talk a bit, and Pete concludes there's no choice but to cut production back. He lays out a new plan, recognizing that there's not much he can do to cut back the May output, since the month is already more than half over:

	FEB	MAR	APR		MAY	JUN	JUL	AUG	SEP
PLANNED PRODUCTION	100	100	100	OLD PLAN	110	120	120	120	120
				NEW PLAN	110	100	100	90	90
ACTUAL PRODUCTION	98	100	101						
DIFFERENCE	−2	—	+1						
CUM DIFFERENCE		−2	−1						

Meanwhile, back in the Finance department, Carol the CFO has just finished a difficult phone call with the company's banker. It centered on such things as excess inventories, poor cash flow, and the need to increase the line of credit. Carol promised the banker that she personally would dig into these problems and get them fixed.

She takes a look at her finished goods inventory report and soon comes across the page for Medium Consumer Widgets:

	FEB	MAR	APR	MAY	JUN	JUL	AUG	SEP
PLANNED INVENTORY (1-MO SUPPLY)	100	100	100	110	120	120	120	120
ACTUAL INVENTORY	103	111	116	132				
DIFFERENCE	+3	+11	+16	+32				

Carol's concerned about the inventory build-up on Medium Consumer Widgets. They now have 132,000 units in stock, which is much higher than the budgeted one-month supply. At a standard cost of $50 each, that's $1,600,000 over plan. She calls Pete at the plant: *Pete, the inventory of Medium Widgets is way up there — 30 percent above authorized. Are you guys working on bringing that down? If so, can I count on the inventory starting to drop?*

Pete replies, *Carol, you don't know the half of it. It's a lot worse than your numbers are showing.* He tells her about Mike's downward forecast revision, and they arrange to meet that afternoon. Later, at their meeting, Pete shows Carol Mike's new forecast and his new production plan.

Mike's Forecast:

	FEB	MAR	APR		MAY	JUN	JUL	AUG	SEP
FORECAST	100	100	100	NEW FORECAST	90	90	90	90	90
ACTUAL SALES	90	95	85						
DIFFERENCE	−10	−5	−15						
CUM DIFFERENCE		−15	−30						

Pete's Production Plan:

	FEB	MAR	APR		MAY	JUN	JUL	AUG	SEP
PLANNED PRODUCTION	100	100	100	NEW PLAN	110	100	100	90	90
ACTUAL PRODUCTION	98	100	101						
DIFFERENCE	−2	—	+1						
CUM DIFFERENCE		−2	−1						

Carol, fearing the worst, picks up a pencil and calculates the projected inventory out into the future. She does this by starting with the 132 finished inventory balance at the end of April, subtracting the sales forecast for each month, and adding in Pete's planned production. Here's what she comes up with:

	APR	*MAY*	*JUN*	*JUL*	*AUG*	*SEP*
INV.	*132*	*152*	*162*	*172*	*172*	*172*

Carol's response: *Good grief! This is awful. The inventory's going over 170,000 — and staying there! That's almost twice as much as we need. At $50 each, we're going to have $8 and a half million tied up in Medium Widgets. Our budget for all finished goods is $10 million. What's going on here?*

Hey, don't blame me, counters Pete. *I just got the new forecast this morning. Seems to me they should have called those numbers down months ago. I've been saying for a long time that the Product Managers don't look at the forecasts often enough.*

Carol: *Pete, I'm afraid you'll need to cut production back a lot more than what you've got here. We just can't live with that inventory.*

Pete: *Well, if we gotta then we gotta. But that means a layoff, which not only costs money but will really drag down morale. And when morale goes down, so does productivity.*

Carol: *I'll get this on the agenda for Monday's executive staff meeting and we can present the issue then. In the meantime, I'll touch base with Mike to see if maybe they can do something to jack up sales.*

What's Wrong with This Picture?

A lot. Let's give some constructive criticism to Mike, Pete, and Carol:

- Mike's not reviewing his forecasts frequently enough. A once-per-quarter review simply isn't adequate for most businesses; they're too fast-paced, too dynamic, too subject to change.

- As a result, demand and supply have become way out of balance. Pete, the plant manager, is faced with a severe cutback in output rates and a likely layoff.

- The activities are disconnected. Each person is looking at his or her part of the business, but nowhere is the entire picture being brought together. The CFO, Carol, is in this particular loop only because the bank has been hassling her.

- The problem is sufficiently serious that Carol will escalate it to the executive staff meeting. This will most likely consume a fair amount of time, be a difficult discussion, and include some finger-pointing and fault-finding. It will not tend to enhance teamwork among the top management team.

Bottom line: Acme Widgets lacks a process to routinely review the status of demand and supply, and to make timely informed decisions about keeping them in balance. What they're lacking is a process like Sales & Operations Planning.

A Better Way to Look at It

Let's pretend for a moment that Acme was just beginning to implement S&OP. Sally Smith, the sales administration manager, is heading up the implementation project and she has just put together an S&OP spreadsheet for Medium Consumer Widgets, a Make-to-Stock product family. Here's what it might look like.

	FEB	MAR	APR	MAY	JUN	JUL	AUG	SEP
FORECAST	100	100	100	100	120	120	120	120
ACTUAL SALES	90	95	85					
DIFFERENCE	−10	−5	−15					
CUM DIFFERENCE		−15	−30					
PLANNED PRODUCTION	100	100	100	110	120	120	120	120
ACTUAL PRODUCTION	98	100	101					
DIFFERENCE	−2	—	+1					
CUM DIFFERENCE		−2	−1					
PLANNED INVENTORY								
(1-MO SUPPLY)	100	100	100	142	142	142	142	142
ACTUAL INV (JAN=103)	111	116	132					
DIFFERENCE	+11	+16	+32					

Let's examine this display for a moment. Notice how both the demand and supply pictures are shown adjacent to each other. They're followed by the inventory projection, which in effect is the critique of the demand/supply relationship.

The result is a holistic picture of the status of the product family. This kind of display contains information specific to each of the three key functions: forecasts and actual sales performance for Sales, the production plan and performance to that plan for Operations, and the inventory status and outlook for the people in Finance, among others.

Each function can view not only its own numbers but also those from other areas. That makes it much easier for managers from a variety of functions to view the business as an organic whole, rather than looking only at their part of it. In the example above, we can see the inventory growth far above plan. We can also track back to the cause: actual sales below forecast. If Sally Smith and her colleagues at Acme Widget had been looking at these numbers every month, they would have been able to *take action sooner* — and not have had to deal with such a major problem as the one they're now facing.

One of the early users of S&OP was the U.S. Pharmaceutical Division of Abbott Labs. Its president stated, *Marketing can challenge Production proposals, Finance can question advertising concepts, and all disciplines participate in the finalization of the production rate proposed by Materials Management. My goal is to get everyone seeing the business through my glasses.*[1]

---

[1] "Game Planning," by David Rucinski. *Production and Inventory Management Journal,* First Quarter 1982, pp. 63 − 68.

S&OP is a monthly process that involves both middle management and the executive group. It's done in aggregate groupings (families, categories), not in detail. For each of a half-dozen to a dozen major product families, the process focuses on a review of:

- **Recent past performance.** It compares actual performance against plan for sales, production, customer service (on-time shipments), inventory or customer order backlog — and highlights the deviations. This visibility into past performance highlights bias and enhances accountability, and those can be major benefits. The future plans represent commitments by Sales and by Operations; the actual numbers show how well they did in hitting those plans. In a number of companies, I've seen this fact alone help reduce the gap between plan and actual performance.

- **The outlook for the future.** New, updated Sales Forecasts and the resulting Operations Plans[2] are developed, modified where necessary, and authorized. (The Operations Plan is the Sales Forecast plus or minus changes in inventories or backlog to meet the customer service targets, seasonal requirements, plant shutdowns, and so forth.)

The Make-to-Stock View

An important aspect of S&OP is the ability to focus on customer service and its interplay with inventories (or customer order backlogs for a purely Make-to-Order business). See Figure 3-1, which is a somewhat simplified example of an S&OP spreadsheet. This spreadsheet shows the three prior months' sales and production performance, the finished goods inventory, and the customer service levels achieved. We can see that sales have exceeded forecast by 44,000 units (over three months), and this has reduced the finished goods inventories to an unacceptably low level. Why unacceptably low? Because customer service is plummeting. It's nowhere near the target of 99 percent.

The forward decisions will then focus on:

- the possibility of an increase to the Sales Forecast,

- how quickly production can gear up to get the inventories back to their target level, and

- actions that can be taken in the short run to minimize the negative impacts of the sub-par customer service levels.

---

[2] Throughout this book, I'll use the term *Operations Plan* rather than *Production Plan* because it's more inclusive and more representative of the operational environment here in the twenty-first century.

Figure 3-1   THE ACME WIDGET COMPANY — SALES & OPERATIONS PLAN FOR OCT 2004

FAMILY: MEDIUM WIDGETS (MAKE-TO-STOCK)   UNIT OF MEASURE: 1000 UNITS

TARGET LINE FILL: 99%   TARGET FINISHED INV: 10 DAYS ON HAND

	HISTORY									3rd 3 MOS	4th 3 MOS	12 MO TOTAL	MOS 13-18	FISCAL YR LATEST CALL	BUS PLAN
SALES	J	A	S	O	N	D	J	F	M						
NEW FORECAST	200	200	200	210	210	220	220	220	220	690	690	2670	1335	$25,540M	$25,400M
ACTUAL SALES	222	195	227												
DIFF: MONTH	22	-5	27												
CUM		17	44												
OPERATIONS															
NEW PLAN	200	200	200	210	220	230	230	230	230	690	690	2735			
ACTUAL	200	206	199												
DIFF: MONTH	0	6	-1												
CUM		6	5												
INVENTORY															
PLAN	100	100	100	61	71	81	91	101	111	111	111				
ACTUAL	78	89	61												
DAYS ON HAND	8	9	6	6	6	7	8	9	10	10	9				
LINE FILL %	97%	98%	89%												

DEMAND ISSUES AND ASSUMPTIONS

1. FORECAST REFLECTS LAUNCH OF NEW DESIGNER WIDGET LINE IN 3RD QTR.

2. ASIA FORECASTED TO REACH 2001 VOLUME

SUPPLY ISSUES

1. XMAS FULL PLANT SHUTDOWN RESCHEDULED TO STAGGERED PARTIALS THRU FALL AND WINTER

One of the important things we've learned from quality improvement initiatives like Six Sigma or TQM is that *facts are our friends*. Sales & Operations Planning gets all of the relevant facts on one sheet of paper. This helps to avoid suboptimal decisions, where one aspect of the business is improved at a disproportionate cost to another. For example, decisions are sometimes made by looking solely at inventory levels, and the outcome is a mandate to cut production in order to get the inventories down. Several months later the customer service statistics show horrible performance, so the word goes out to crank up production so we can start to ship on time. And on and on.

S&OP avoids this by displaying planned and actual data for sales, production, inventories, and most important, customer service — all on the same page. In my experience, executives find this very helpful, because it helps them make better decisions.

Please notice that this display goes out 18 months into the future. This is to enable both efficient budgeting and effective capacity planning, which we'll talk more about in Chapter 10. We'll use an 18-month forward planning horizon in all our examples.

One last point: Many S&OP spreadsheets show the number of production days in each month, which helps to explain month-to-month variability. Most of the spreadsheet examples in this book do not do so, for reasons of clarity and ease of understanding. A spreadsheet showing work days (production days) is shown in Chapter 13.

The Make-to-Order View

First, let's contrast Make-to-Stock with Make-to-Order. Make-to-stock says, "Make the product and then wait for the customer orders to come in." In essence, Make-to-Order says, "Wait for the orders to come in and then start to make the product." Make-to-order, at least within the context of S&OP, refers to companies that do *very little* work on the product prior to receipt of the customer order.[3]

There are two gray areas here:

• Some companies make products that are specific to only one customer. This sounds like Make-to-Order. However, for contractual or other reasons, they must carry a finished inventory for a given customer. Big-Mart might be saying: "We want you to always have two weeks' supply of our products in your warehouse." For S&OP purposes, this is not a Make-to-Order situation but rather it's Make-to-Stock, because the products flow through a finished goods inventory.

• Some companies *finish* products after receipt of the customer order, using standard components. For S&OP, this also is not Make-to-Order but rather Finish-to-Order, and we'll cover that later in this chapter.

The logic of Sales & Operations Planning for Make-to-Order products is *almost* identical to make-tostock. The big difference, as shown in Figure 3-2, is that the finished goods inventory is no longer in the picture but is replaced by the customer order backlog.

"Backlog" refers to all customer orders received but not yet shipped, regardless of when they're due to ship. It's actually "negative inventory." Finished goods inventory is what has been produced ahead of receiving customer orders for it. Backlog represents orders received ahead of producing the products.

---

[3] A subset of Make-to-Order is called *Design-to-Order* or *Engineer-to-Order*. This is for products whose detailed design is not even begun until receipt of the customer order. Products in this category tend to be large, specialized, complex machinery — often one of a kind. For S&OP, this is treated in much the same way as Make-to-Order.

Figure 3-2	THE ACME WIDGET COMPANY — SALES & OPERATIONS PLAN FOR OCT 2004
FAMILY:	LARGE WIDGETS (MAKE-TO-ORDER) UNIT OF MEASURE: EACH
TARGET LINE FILL:	99% TARGET ORDER BACKLOG: 6 WEEKS

	HISTORY									3rd 3 MOS	4th 3 MOS	12 MO TOTAL	MOS 13-18	FISCAL YR LATEST CALL	BUS PLAN
BOOKINGS	J	A	S	O	N	D	J	F	M						
NEW FORECAST	20	20	20	20	20	20	20	20	20	60	60	240	120	$1,800M	$1,800M
ACTUAL BOOKINGS	22	20	21	20	10	4									
DIFF: MONTH	2	0	1												
CUM		2	3												
PRODUCTION/SHIPMENTS															
NEW PLAN	20	20	20	20	20	20	20	20	20	60	60	240	120		
ACTUAL	20	21	20												
DIFF: MONTH	0	1	0												
CUM		1	1												
ORDER BACKLOG															
PLAN	30	30	30	30	30	30	30	30	30	30	30				
ACTUAL 28	30	29	30												
BACKLOG — # WEEKS 6	6	6	6	6	6	6	6	6	6	6					
ORDER FILL % 99%	100%	100%													

DEMAND ISSUES AND ASSUMPTIONS   **SUPPLY ISSUES**

1. FORECAST ASSUMES NO CHANGE IN
   COMPETITOR PRICING OR BACKLOG

The size of the customer order backlog can be an important competitive factor. The backlog is a primary determiner of lead time to customers because the bigger the backlog, the longer the lead time. If the backlog gets too big and hence the lead times get too long, then the customers might not want to wait. They may go somewhere else where they can get the product sooner. If the backlog gets too small, Operations and possibly other departments can have problems; there may not be enough work to stay efficient. Sales & Operations Planning helps Make-to-Order manufacturers manage the size of their customer order backlogs; thanks to S&OP's superior visibility, it's easier to keep those backlogs where they should be.

Here's an example. Let's imagine that Acme Widget salespeople see an opportunity in the marketplace: if they could cut their lead times from six weeks to four, they feel they would capture business from the competition. Operations agrees that this is practical and lays out a plan to cut the backlog by two weeks. The resulting plan, which could easily become a formal recommendation to the executive group, might look like Figure 3-3. Operations is committing to a temporary 15 percent ramp-up in production, from 20 units per month to 23. They could possibly ramp up higher and thus reach the four-week backlog target sooner, but as the supply comment points out, this plan is conservative and cost-effective. Starting in March, the plan is to drop back to 21 and then 20. Of course, the hope is that the new four-week customer lead time will get more business and thus Acme might not have to drop back at all from 23 per month.

Figure 3-3 THE ACME WIDGET COMPANY — SALES & OPERATIONS PLAN FOR OCT 2004

FAMILY: LARGE WIDGETS (MAKE-TO-ORDER)   UNIT OF MEASURE: EACH

TARGET LINE FILL: 99%   **TARGET ORDER BACKLOG: 4 WEEKS**

	HISTORY			O	N	D	J	F	M	3rd 3 MOS	4th 3 MOS	12 MO TOTAL	MOS 13-18	FISCAL YR LATEST CALL	BUS PLAN
BOOKINGS	J	A	S												
NEW FORECAST	20	20	20	20	20	20	20	20	20	60	60	240	120	$1,800M	$1,800M
ACTUAL BOOKINGS	22	20	21	20	10	4									
DIFF: MONTH	2	0	1												
CUM		2	3												
PRODUCTION/SHIPMENTS															
OLD PLAN	20	20	20	20	20	20	20	20	20	60	60	240	120		
NEW PLAN				20	21	22	23	23	21	60	60	250	120		
ACTUAL	20	21	20												
DIFF: MONTH	0	1	0												
CUM		1	1												
ORDER BACKLOG															
OLD PLAN	30	30	30	30	30	30	30	30	30	30	30				
NEW PLAN				30	29	27	24	21	20	20	20				
ACTUAL	28	30	29	30												
BACKLOG — # WEEKS	6	6	6	6	6	5	5	4	4	4	4				
ORDER FILL %	99%	100%	100%												

DEMAND ISSUES AND ASSUMPTIONS

1. FORECAST ASSUMES NO CHANGE IN COMPETITOR PRICING OR BACKLOG

2. FORECAST DOES NOT REFLECT INCREASED SALES DUE TO SHORTER BACKLOG

SUPPLY ISSUES

1. PRODUCTION RAMP-UP TO REACH 4-WK BACKLOG IS CONSERVATIVE BUT COST-EFFECTIVE

The Finish-to-Order View (Postponement)

Does the word "postponement" ring a bell? How about the phrase "mass customization"? Ever hear about — or perhaps experience — Dell Computer's highly successful "build-to-order" strategy? Well, all of these terms are getting at much the same thing: finishing the product to the customer's specifications *only after receipt* of the customer order. But there's more: the product needs to be finished and shipped *quickly*, within a few days, so the customers don't wait long at all to get their products. This contrasts with a standard Make-to-Order process, which most often involves order fulfillment times of weeks or months, not days.

Let's stay with the Dell Computer example since most of us are familiar with that company. If you want to buy a computer from Dell, you can't have them ship one to you off the shelf. That's because they don't carry a stock of finished computers.

They do, however, have all the components necessary to make their computers readily available. When the customer order arrives, they create a bill of material which specifies which options the customer has selected: things like processor speed, amount of RAM, screen size, and so forth. They then *finish* the product using these available components.

Dell calls this approach "build-to-order." Other companies use the term *finish to order*, and that's what we'll call it in this book. Similar terms include assemble-to-order, package-to-order, late-stage differentiation, blend-to-order (in chemicals), and perhaps the one most frequently used — postponement.

Well, is this Finish-to-Order approach a good thing? In most cases, it definitely is. It can drive customer service up to very high levels and simultaneously reduce the finished goods inventory to near zero. It can be particularly helpful in companies whose products have lots of options and are under pressure to ship quickly. To follow a Make-to-Stock strategy in a case like this is difficult, because of high finished inventories coupled frequently with poor customer service (because the forecasts of the many individual items are almost always wrong).

Some people have difficulty understanding how S&OP can support Finish-to-Order. Unlike Make-to-Stock, there is normally no finished inventory and hence, no finished inventory target of days' supply. Unlike Make-to-Order, the customer order backlog is at or near zero; the goal is to ship very soon after receipt of the order. So what can serve as the target value if not finished inventory or order backlog?

The key to Finish-to-Order is to produce quickly using *available* components. Only by having the components readily accessible can production occur quickly. Therefore, the target is the size of the *component* inventory available to be used in the finishing operations. It's normally expressed in day's supply, and often employs a key component — one might think of it as a surrogate — to represent the total component inventory. Here are some examples:

• A manufacturer of electronic products keys on "modules." They try to keep several days' supply of each of their various key modules ready for production. Their purchasing and fabrication processes — for power supplies, housings, sensors, packaging, and so on — are tied to this surrogate target in their Master Schedule; if not, they might run out or have too much.

• A chemical company, in its latex division, targets its inventory of primary product prior to final blending. Given the right amount of primary product, it's able to blend to order quickly and on-time — and to complete its "packaging" operation, which is to fill tanker trucks and rail cars.

• A company making tape has its S&OP process focused on the number of "rolls." These are the wide rolls of tape, in about ten different colors, prior to slitting (width) and cutting (length). Upon receipt of the customer order, they quickly slit, cut, package, and ship. Here, the surrogate (rolls) drives the planning for components (packaging, cores, and so forth) via the Master Schedule; some of these items are replenished via a demand-pull, Kanban process and others via supplier scheduling.

Please note: in all of these examples, they are not keying on finished inventory. There is little or none of that, and that's the way they want it. They do need availability of components, and that's where they have S&OP focused.

In Figure 3-4, we see an S&OP spreadsheet for a Finish-to-Order product family, calling for a target module inventory of five days on hand. Note the section labeled Module Inventory. In September, the module inventory dropped to three days on hand and customer service dropped. Consequently, the Operations Plan for the next several months has been set higher than the Sales Forecast to build the module inventory up to the five-day target.

Please note: all of the above data relative to sales, operations, and module inventory must be in the same unit of measure. Sometimes the nature of the surrogate is such that it must be expressed in a unit of measure different from that of the sales forecast. In those cases, the sales forecast is usually converted into the surrogate's unit of measure and is shown accordingly.

For example, sales forecast for the tape manufacturer cited above might be expressed in cases, while the surrogate (rolls) is expressed in linear feet. What's needed here is to convert cases to feet and to show that on the S&OP spreadsheet. Some companies will show both in the Sales area (cases and feet of rolls, in our example) but do the arithmetic using the surrogate unit of measure, because that's how the Operations Plan and Inventory are shown.

Figure 3-4 THE ACME WIDGET COMPANY — SALES & OPERATIONS PLAN FOR OCT 2004

FAMILY: DESIGNER WIDGETS (FINISH-TO-ORDER) UNIT OF MEASURE: EACH

TARGET LINE FILL: 99.9% TARGET MODULE INV: 5 DAYS ON HAND

SALES	H I S T O R Y J	A	S	O	N	D	J	F	M	3rd 3 MOS AVG	4th 3 MOS AVG	12 MO TOTAL AVG	NEXT 6 MOS AVG	FISCAL YR LATEST CALL	BUS PLAN
NEW FORECAST	2000	2000	2000	2100	2200	2200	2200	2200	2200	2300	2300	2400	2500	$51,080M	$50,800M
ACTUAL SALES	2220	1950	2270												
DIFF: MONTH	220	-50	270											MARGIN: 33.0%	32.5%
CUM		170	440												

OPERATIONS															
NEW PLAN	2000	2000	2000	2200	2300	2200	2200	2200	2300	2300	2300	2450	2500	$34,250M	$34,290M
ACTUAL	2000	2060	1990												
DIFF: MONTH	0	60	-10												
CUM		60	50												

MODULE INV.															
PLAN	500	500	500	410	510	510	510	510	610	610	610			$9083M	$9125M
ACTUAL	480	590	310												
DAYS ON HAND	5	6	3	4	5	5	5	5	6	6	6				
LINE FILL %	99.5%	100%	98.7%												

DEMAND ISSUES AND ASSUMPTIONS

1. HOUSING STARTS FORECASTED FLAT FOR NEXT YEAR

2. WILL START SHIPPING BIG-MART 10/20

3. MARKET SHARE PROJECTED +5% BY SUMMER

SUPPLY ISSUES

1. WILL BEGIN SOURCING MODULES 3A, 4A, & 4B FROM ASIA 12/1

The View for Seasonal Products

Acme Widget has a line of products — Christmas Widgets — with a highly seasonal sales curve. Over three-quarters of the total year's sales for Christmas Widgets are shipped during September, October, and November. Here's next year's sales forecast for Christmas Widgets, in thousands:

J	F	M	A	M	J	J	A	S	O	N	D
0	0	0	0	0	0	0	100	300	400	300	100 = 1,200

Acme doesn't have enough capacity to produce such a large volume in just a few months, feeling that having that much capacity would not be cost-effective. Therefore, they must produce early in order to meet their customers' demand. They start this early production, called the "pre-build," in April.

Obviously, this has the effect of building inventory sharply during the period April – August, and thus the concept of a single, fixed-quantity finished inventory target doesn't work here. Over the summer, the inventory will be increasing to a quite high level — by design. At the end of the selling season, Acme would like to have nothing left in inventory in order to avoid the costs of carrying it over until the next season. Thus, a seasonal inventory target that builds up based on a defined maximum and then falls to a defined minimum at the end of the season is far more valid. This is shown in Figure 3-5.

Figure 3-5	THE ACME WIDGET COMPANY — SALES & OPERATIONS PLAN FOR OCT 2004
FAMILY: CHRISTMAS WIDGETS (MAKE-TO-STOCK)	UNIT OF MEASURE: 1000 UNITS
TARGET LINE FILL: 97%	TARGET FIN INV (WEEKS): MAX: 20, END: 0

	HISTORY										3rd	4th	12 MO	MOS	FISCAL YR	BUS
SALES	M	A	M	J	J	A	S	O	N	D	3 MOS	3 MOS	TOTAL	13-18	LATEST CALL	PLAN
NEW FORECAST	0	0	0	0	0	100	300	400	300	100	0	0	1200	400	$10,800M	$10,800M
ACTUAL SALES	0	0	0	0												
DIFF: MONTH																
CUM																
OPERATIONS																
NEW PLAN	0	80	100	120	140	160	200	200	200	0	0	300	1200	500		
ACTUAL	0	73	104	123												
DIFF: MONTH	0	-7	4	3												
CUM			-3	0												
INVENTORY (F.G)																
NEW PLAN	0	80	180	300	440	500	400	200	100	0	0	300				
ACTUAL	0	73	177	300												
WEEKS ON HAND	0	16	13	11	9	6	4	3	4	0						
LINE FILL %																

DEMAND ISSUES AND ASSUMPTIONS

1. ANTICIPATING LATER ORDERS THAN LAST YEAR, AND MORE FOLLOW-ON ORDERS IN DECEMBER

SUPPLY ISSUES

1. WILL BE ABLE TO CONTINUE PRODUCTION ONE OR TWO WEEKS INTO DECEMBER

Note the target finished goods inventory in the upper right part of the display: a maximum of 20 weeks' supply with a desired inventory at year end of zero. The plan as laid out accomplished those directives, with the inventory rising to 16 weeks' worth early in the pre-build and sold out by December.

Operations Plan Choices:
Level, Chase, or Hybrid

Broadly, there are three choices when laying out the Operations Plan:

- Produce (or procure) at a level rate all year, called, appropriately, a *level* strategy.

- Set the Operations Plan to match the Sales Forecast, called a *chase* strategy.

- Do a combination of the two, a *hybrid* approach.

In actual practice, most companies use the hybrid approach, as in the case of the Christmas Widgets at Acme. In other words, they will do some chasing of the sales curve while trying to maintain a reasonably level production rate.

Lean Manufacturing calls for a level rate, but only in the short run. In practice, many Lean shops find that the demand picture for their families changes as they move through the year, and hence employ either a chase or a hybrid strategy, adjusting their leveled schedules upwards or downwards to reflect volume changes in increments, such as month to month. For highly seasonal products, trying to produce at a level rate all year could generate a great deal of inventory. This would qualify as waste, and thus it runs directly counter to the principles of Lean Manufacturing. This then, is another example of needing a chase or at least a hybrid strategy.

We'll return to the issue of the S&OP spreadsheet in Chapter 10, when we'll get into the nitty-gritty of spreadsheet design, formulas, and enhancements to what we've seen here, including some thoughts on how to display the information via graphs as opposed to the purely numerical tables that we've seen thus far.

FREQUENTLY ASKED QUESTIONS

Why do the Make-to-Stock and Finish-to-Order spreadsheets show finished goods or component inventory only? What about raw materials and work-in-process (WIP)?

Several reasons, one being that they're not an integral part of the S&OP logic, which focuses on the interplay between demand, supply, and the level of finished goods, order backlog, or key components.

There are other tools available to manage raw material and WIP inventories: Master Scheduling, Kanban, MRP, and Plant and Supplier Scheduling. These processes take their marching orders — directly or indirectly — from S&OP.

Another reason is that often it's impossible to tie the raw-material inventory to specific product families. A given raw material may go into a number of different product families. On the other hand, if you can segregate the data validly, there's nothing wrong with displaying raw material and WIP numbers on the spreadsheet as memo entries, provided it would add value and not just clutter.

Chapter 4

Inputs to S&OP

The two major inputs to Sales & Operations Planning are, quite simply, demand and supply. That figures, because S&OP's job is to help people get demand and supply in balance — and to keep them in balance.

Demand Input: Sales Forecasting

In some companies, the toughest part of implementing Sales & Operations Planning is overcoming an aversion to forecasting. Let's look at five fundamental questions that surround this problem.

Why Bother with Forecasting?

It's amazing, but I still hear this question from time to time. Often it comes from the same people who say, "You can't forecast this business."

My response is Nuts. Of course the business can be forecasted — perhaps not with great accuracy, but it certainly can be done. As a matter of fact, virtually all businesses do a significant degree of forecasting. (The only ones who don't are those whose order fulfillment time to their customers is *longer* than their total lead time to get material and capacity. Have you seen many of those lately?)

The problem in many companies is that people in Operations do the "forecasting" by default, i.e., they order the long-lead-time materials and release the long-lead-time production items. Not having a forecast, they must guess. Unfortunately, most of those folks aren't close to the customers; they don't know about Sales' plans for promotions, pricing, sales force incentives, and the like; and thus they rely heavily on history rather than on the future outlook in the marketplace. When things go wrong, it reinforces the beliefs of the people who are saying, "You can't forecast this business. See? I told you so."

Point 1: Forecasting is being done in virtually every company. The issues are who does it and at what level it's done. I'll have more to say later about this last point, the level at which forecasting is done. For now, let me just say that most companies do too much forecasting at the detail level, and not enough at higher, more aggregated levels.

Who Owns the Forecast?

Who's responsible for it? Who actually does the forecasting? In many companies, when I ask these questions, crisp answers rarely come back. I hear things like "it depends which forecast you're talking about" or "well, it's not very clear" or "it doesn't matter, because we use the forecast only for budgeting; we run the business on past history and hunches."

That's too bad, because a good way to increase customer service levels and reduce inventories simultaneously is to do a first-rate job of forecasting. And in order to do a first-rate job, we'd better have clarity on whose job it is.

The issue here is accountability, and the underlying principle is this: the people responsible for developing the plan (in this case the forecast, the demand plan) should be the same ones who will be held accountable for executing the plan.

Thus, **Point 2: Sales and Marketing people "own" the Sales Forecast.** It's their job; they're the experts on the demand side of the business, in both planning and execution. People in other departments may support them, perhaps by operating the statistical forecasting system or otherwise generating basic data. But it's the job of the Sales and Marketing folks to review, update, and modify the Sales Forecast; they own it. They own it, because they *sell* it.[1] They're the company's primary contact with the customers, who are — after all — the drivers of demand.

How Accurate Should the Forecast Be?

When people ask me this question, I wince. I try never to use the word *forecast* and the word *accurate* in the same sentence. Why? Because it's a turnoff for the folks in Sales who will be called upon to do the forecasting.

People who routinely criticize the forecasters for their inaccuracy might ask themselves a few basic questions. First, if the Sales people could predict the future with great accuracy, do you really think they'd be working for a living? Would they be knocking themselves out for forty or fifty or more hours per week? Of course not. If they could predict the future with great accuracy, where would they be? At the racetrack. And if the track were closed? They'd be home on their PCs, trading in stock options and speculating on pork-belly futures.

---

[1] Most of us learned this in Management 101: The people who develop the plan should be the same ones who are accountable for its execution.

Even the best forecasts will almost always be inaccurate to one degree or another. The job of the forecasters is twofold. First, they must get the forecast in the ballpark, good enough to enable Operations people to do a proper job of initial procurement and production, capacity planning, etc. Frequently this does not require forecasts at a detailed level, but works fine with aggregated forecasts — perhaps by product family, subfamily, or brand.

The second major goal for forecasters is continuous improvement in reducing forecast error. In doing this, they are not trying to reach some enchanted nirvana of forecasting perfection, but to routinely produce forecasts that reflect what I call the "four R's of forecasting": forecasts that are reasoned, realistic, reviewed frequently, and represent the total demand.

Forecasting is a process. It has inputs and outputs, just like a production operation. See Figure 4-1, which shows the forecasting process in terms of inputs and outputs. Note the output — forecasts that

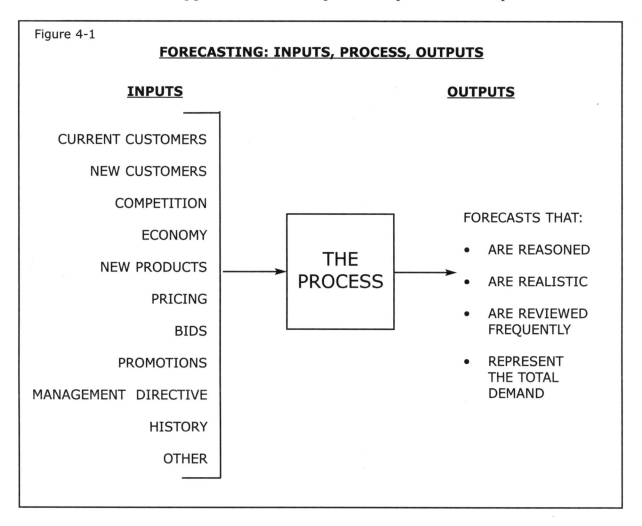

Figure 4-1

FORECASTING: INPUTS, PROCESS, OUTPUTS

INPUTS

CURRENT CUSTOMERS

NEW CUSTOMERS

COMPETITION

ECONOMY

NEW PRODUCTS

PRICING

BIDS

PROMOTIONS

MANAGEMENT DIRECTIVE

HISTORY

OTHER

THE PROCESS

OUTPUTS

FORECASTS THAT:

• ARE REASONED

• ARE REALISTIC

• ARE REVIEWED FREQUENTLY

• REPRESENT THE TOTAL DEMAND

are reasoned, reasonable, reviewed frequently, and reflect the total demand. Nowhere does it say "accurate" because talking about accuracy clouds and emotionally charges the issue. The issue is the process.

Point 3: Better processes yield better results and forecasting is no exception; better forecasting processes will yield better forecasts. A forecast that's closer to actual demand, one that contains less forecast error, means less inventory in terms of safety stock, reduced expediting, fewer unplanned changes in the plant, and so forth. So although I don't talk about accurate forecasts, I do promote "good" forecasts. Good means that the forecasters are working the process, applying their knowledge of the customers, the marketplace, future sales and marketing plans, and in general doing the best job they can.

Another, probably better, way of saying it comes from Rebecca Morgan of Fulcrum Consulting Works in Cleveland: "*Accuracy* is a term to be avoided. I use the term 'quality' in referring to fitness for use and reduced variability of forecasts over time."

Where Should You Forecast?

I don't mean where physically to forecast, as in "Should we do the forecasting in Joan's office or Doug's? Joan's got a window, but Doug's coffee is better." No, I'm talking about where in the overall product structure to forecast. In other words, at what level should you forecast? Some choices are shown on the adjacent pyramid.

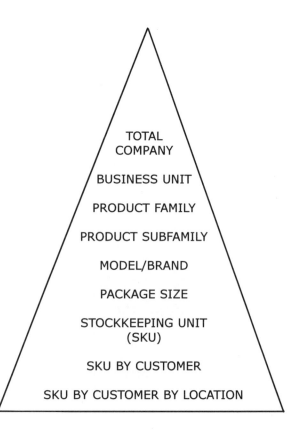

Forecasting at the top of the pyramid won't work. Obviously forecasting only one line item — the total company — won't do the job; it's just not specific enough to provide good direction to Operations and others.

How about forecasting down at the bottom, stockkeeping unit (SKU) by customer by location? Well, it contains all the detail, and it gives you the capability to aggregate upwards in lots of ways. But don't jump to the conclusion that it's the best. It may be *too much* detail; forecasting at this lowest, most detailed level may actually cause more forecast error, not less. One reason is that it fails to take advantage of the law of large numbers (which states that larger numbers are generally easier to forecast). Another reason is that it can be a lot more work.

One company in the spirits business learned that forecasting at the lowest possible level would be counterproductive. There was simply too much unneeded detail. For example, a case of Old Loudmouth Bourbon, 750 ml, going to Pennsylvania is a different SKU from the identical product going to Ohio, because they take different case labels. The company decided it didn't have to forecast SKUs, but rather found it was able to do most of its forecasting at the brand/package size level.

Let me digress for a moment, just in case you're wondering about the supply side of this story. Well, the plants printed their own case labels, with virtually zero lead time. If they were filling an order for Ohio, they'd print Ohio labels. This is a good example of how operational effectiveness — in this case, ultra-short lead times — can make life easier for the forecasters. There's a principle here: "Plan the volume; manage the mix." When you can finish products very quickly, adding the optionality at the end of the production cycle, you can often get out of the business of forecasting mix and focus on volumes.

So you should not necessarily forecast at the most detailed level possible. Higher may be better. On the other hand, it's best to *store* the data — both actual data and forecast — at the lowest level possible, which in some companies means storing by stockkeeping unit by customer by location. That makes it possible to capture and retain very specific demand for certain customers and to view it when necessary.

For example, in the case cited above, let's say that the state of Ohio had decided to have an aggressive promotion on Old Loudmouth Bourbon, 750 ml, from April through June; they anticipate that sales will be 300 percent of normal during that period. It's important to get that kind of intelligence into your formal forecasting system on a rigorous and managed basis.

Many companies are able to forecast effectively at the family or subfamily level, and that's a good place to be. Lean Manufacturing can be particularly helpful here: as lead times get very short, thanks to Lean, it becomes possible to finish and ship the product very quickly after receipt of the customer order. The need for detailed forecasting goes away. This is one example among many of how Lean Manufacturing simplifies the operating environment and thus the planning and scheduling tools needed to control that environment become simpler. Lean can make the forecasting job much less difficult.

Some companies, however, do need to forecast at a somewhat lower level and then roll up the detail to subfamilies and families. However, they should do this *only* out through a point in time called the Planning Time Fence, which defines the cumulative lead time — for material and production — of the product. Beyond that, it's far better to forecast at an aggregated, family or subfamily level.[2]

How Frequently Should You Forecast?

For a formal review, a good frequency is once per month. Of course, if the demand picture undergoes major changes mid-month, the forecast should be updated at that time. Forecasting less frequently than once per month can lead to the kind of problem that Mike, Pete, and Carol faced in Chapter 3.

Forecasting more frequently than once per month can work well, but before you jump into that, be sure you're doing it for the right reason. I've seen companies changing the forecast very frequently in order to effect changes directly into the near-term production line-up. Almost always this is a result of not having a good scheduling system, so they manipulate the forecast (a statement of demand) to directly affect production, which of course is supply. It is not a good practice, and it almost never yields good results.

Company S produces consumer packaged goods with a highly seasonal sales curve. They used to change the forecast frequently, in the very near term. What do you think the impact was on the plants? It drove them crazy. There were constant changes: stop that, start this, increase that, decrease this. As I learned more about what they were doing, I saw why: their master scheduling and plant scheduling processes were right out of the 1950s. The sales and marketing folks felt their only chance of getting the right stuff produced was to constantly change the forecast. It was the informational equivalent of using a saw to drive nails.

The good news is they don't do that anymore. They have a good resource planning system in place and can really manage their Master Schedule and plant schedules. Today they change the forecast far less frequently, run the plant more efficiently, and provide far better customer service than before.

On the other hand, some companies who excel at Continuous Replenishment (CR)[3] update their "forecasts" a number of times per week. Typically they're receiving point-of-sale data from their larger customers, and thus can see through the customers' distribution systems right into the retail

---

[2] For more on this topic, see Thomas F. Wallace and Robert A. Stahl, *Sales Forecasting: A New Approach*, Cincinnati, OH: T.F. Wallace & Company, 2002.

[3] This is a subset of a group of processes known as *Efficient Consumer Response,* which is used widely in the consumer packaged goods field. CR is aimed at very rapid replenishment of the retailers' inventories, based on receiving timely sales data from the retail stores.

stores. They can recalculate their customers' expected demands over the next few days, reset their finishing schedules, and produce.

This is beyond the scope of most companies' capabilities today. Unless you're really good at it, or have an overriding need, go with a frequency of once per month for your forecast updates. It fits nicely with the S&OP cycle, and you can always go to a greater forecast frequency later if it will help you balance demand and supply at the mix level.

The Supply View: Capacity

The job of the people in Operations is to evaluate the new Operations Plan for "doability." Can we hit the numbers called for in the plan, or do they represent ten pounds of potatoes in a five-pound bag? Or maybe two pounds in that five-pound bag? This is a critical step, because what's needed here is either an Operations commitment to hit the numbers in the Operations Plan or, if that's not possible, a revised Operations Plan that can be accomplished. In the latter case, if the doable Operations Plan is not adequate to support the Sales Forecast, then this issue is carried into the Pre-SOP meeting, described in the next chapter.

In some companies, evaluating a plan is easy; in others, it's more involved — and it's determined by how production resources line up with product families. We need to spend a little time here talking about how production facilities are organized.

Aligned Resources

In some cases, the production departments match up closely with the product families — Product A is made in Department A, Product B in Department B. In this situation, the capacity check can be performed right on the S&OP spreadsheet itself. Since there's a one-to-one relationship between product family and production resource, the Operations Plan for that product family represents the entire workload for the resource. The Operations people know what rates they can hit, or can gear up to hit, and it's all visible on one piece of paper. I refer to this kind of organization of manufacturing facilities as "aligned," i.e., the resources are closely aligned with the product families.

Matrix (Nonaligned) Resources

In some companies, there is no tight match-up between product families and resources. A schematic of these two different approaches is shown in Figure 4-2.

The Acme Widget Company had nonaligned resources. Both of their primary product categories — Industrial and Consumer — were made in the same departments in their plant: Fabrication 1, Fabrication 2, Subassembly, and Final Assembly. A further complication was that the low end of the small and medium consumer widget families was outsourced, i.e., purchased as complete products from an outside supplier.

Try as they might, the Acme people couldn't integrate the "operations view" of the business into their product families without making the whole picture terribly complicated and user-unfriendly. They solved the problem by keeping it simple. They set up the product families and subfamilies by major category (Industrial and Consumer) and by product (small, medium, large), as shown below:

Product Families

Large Industrial Widgets	Large Consumer Widgets
Medium Industrial Widgets	Medium Consumer Widgets
Small Industrial Widgets	Small Consumer Widgets

Resources

Fabrication 1	Subassembly
Fabrication 2	Final Assembly
Contract Manufacturer A (Outsourced Products)	

Please note: some plants have some of each. Some resources are aligned; others not. For example, in some chemical plants, the primary operations (for example, the reactor train) are aligned while the packaging operations are not. Thus the capacity for the reactor train can be done as an aligned resource, but packaging cannot. As a nonaligned resource, packaging needs Rough-Cut Capacity Planning.

Rough-Cut Capacity Planning

The nonaligned resources are separate elements; they represent the *supply* side of the business. Within the family groupings, Acme people first do the forecasting of future demand, and then set the Operations Plan to meet the demand and keep inventories or order backlogs at their desired levels. The Operations Plan for the individual families is then "translated" into units of workload for each resource, using a process called "Rough-Cut Capacity Planning."[4]

---

[4] This is an instance in which I deviate from standard APICS terminology. The APICS Dictionary uses several terms: *Rough-Cut Capacity Planning* refers to capacity planning in conjunction with the Master Schedule; *Resource Planning* and *Resource Requirements Planning* specify the process when used at the higher, Operations Plan level. Consistent with my belief that fewer terms are better, I use *Rough-Cut* in both contexts, since the logic and process steps are much the same.

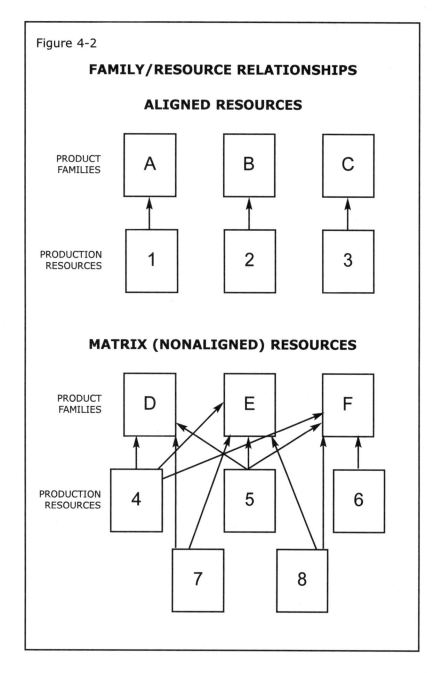

Figure 4-2

FAMILY/RESOURCE RELATIONSHIPS

ALIGNED RESOURCES

PRODUCT FAMILIES

PRODUCTION RESOURCES

MATRIX (NONALIGNED) RESOURCES

PRODUCT FAMILIES

PRODUCTION RESOURCES

This rough-cut process enables the operations people to relate the required capacity (demand) to their available capacity (supply). They're able to evaluate the "doability" of the plan, changes needed in staffing levels, the need for new equipment, and so on.

After the newly updated Operations Plan is rearranged into aggregate departmental workloads and typically translated from units into hours, it must be displayed so that Operations people can see where their problems are.

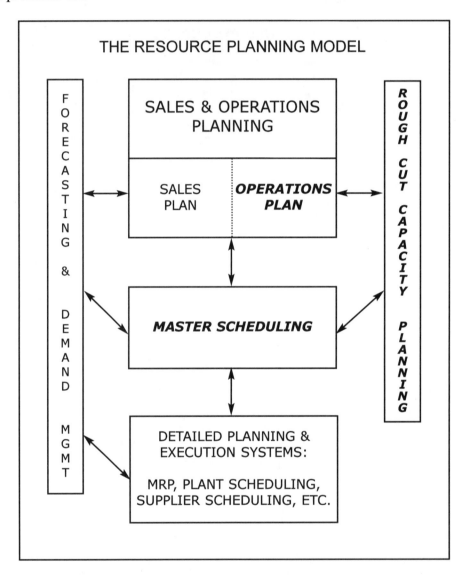

Bills of Resources for Rough-Cut Capacity Planning

The mechanics of Rough-Cut Capacity Planning (RCCP) are straightforward. It requires what are called *Bills of Resources,*[5] a kind of matrix that links product families to key resources. Let's take a look at Figure 4-3, which shows a simplified display from a company making pharmaceuticals.

---

[5] Also called *Load Profiles*

This matrix tells us, among other things, that making 1000 units of product family A will require, on average, 2.7 hours of time in Mixing, 1.2 in Filling, and so forth. The same kind of data is available for the other families, D through F.[6]

Bills of Resources can be developed in several ways:

• By analyzing routings and calculating averages for all products within a family. (A weighted average, based on planned volumes, may be required if there are significant variances in the time requirements of different products within the family.);

• By pulling historical data from job cost records;

• By using estimates from knowledgeable people in Production, Product Engineering, and Purchasing; or

• By using some combination of the above.

Figure 4-3

BILL OF RESOURCES — FAMILY LEVEL (PER 000 UNITS)

KEY RESOURCES	FAMILIES					
DESCRIPTION	A	B	C	D	E	F
MIX (HRS)	2.7	5.0	13.1	—	1.8	14.0
FILL (HRS)	1.2	3.1	2.6	—	11.8	6.0
TEST (HRS)	1.6	2.4	1.1	0.7	—	7.0
LABELER #6 (HRS)	3.3	3.3	—	2.0	—	—
WAREHOUSE SPACE (CUBE)	6.7	3.3	—	2.6	—	19.0
SUPPLIER A (GALLONS)	8.7	6.7	7.1	—	4.2	—

[6] Normally, a typical product for a given family is used to represent the entire family, including a planned run quantity or lot size. This enables set-up and changeover time to be included in the load calculations, which can be significant in a non-Lean environment.

Adding the Operations Plan into the picture enables the calculation of the Rough-Cut Capacity Plan for one month, shown in Figure 4-4.

Figure 4-4

ROUGH-CUT CAPACITY PLAN (ONE MONTH)

KEY RESOURCES	FAMILY PRODUCTION PLAN QUANTITY						CAPACITY		
DESCRIPTION	A	B	C	D	E	F	REQ'D	DEMO	MAX DEMO
	15,000	6,000	21,000	10,000	34,000	6,000			
MIX (HRS)	41	30	275	—	61	84	491	584	621
FILL (HRS)	18	19	55	—	401	36	529	450	482
TEST (HRS)	24	14	23	7	—	42	110	119	146
LABELLER #6 (HRS)	50	20	—	20	—	—	90	77	136
WHSE SPACE (CUBE)	101	20	—	26	—	114	261	370	410
SUPPLIER (GALLONS)	131	40	149	—	143	—	463	500	640

Here we can see the result of multiplying the hours in the Bill of Resources by the amount of the Operations Plan. For example, multiplying Product Family A's 2.7 hours of work required in Mixing by the Operations Plan for Family A — 15,000 units — results in 40.5 hours, rounded to 41. Some interesting information is shown in the three right columns:

- The column headed "Required Capacity," the sum of all the numbers to its left, represents the *demand* for capacity. To accomplish the Operations Plan will require that much output.

- The next column, "Demonstrated Capacity," shows the *supply* of capacity, i.e., how much capacity we have available. Please note the word "demonstrated." This refers to average actual output, often expressed in standard hours: what we have proven we can produce, as opposed to a calculated, theoretical output that we may or may not be able to hit.

• The rightmost column, "Max Demo Capacity," refers an upper limit of output that might be reached with heavy overtime or other means. Many companies will use this as a statement of capacity that can be attained for a relatively short time, not a level they'd like to operate at over the long run.

In Figure 4-4, we can see some problems, an obvious one being Filling. Required Capacity for the month is 529 hours, far in excess of the Demonstrated Capacity or even the Maximum. This says that the Operations Plan as it now stands is not producible. Something has to change, either via increasing the supply of capacity or decreasing the demand for it.

Displaying and Using the Rough-Cut Capacity Information

The information in Figure 4-4 shows the picture on *all* of the resources for only *one month*. In actual practice, it's usually the reverse: A rough-cut display will show only *one resource*, but for a *number of months* into the future. The problem in Filling will become clearer when seen that way, as shown in Figure 4-5. The workload is first compared against demonstrated capacity, both on a month-to-month basis and then cumulatively, and then against *maximum* demonstrated capacity. Using this information, the supply planning people can evaluate the overall load for doability. This resource seems to be capable of doing the overall volume of work if it runs at maximum capacity, and it might make sense to bump up the normal capacity if possible. In addition, some month-to-month overloads, including one in month 1, will need to be worked out — possibly by rescheduling, possibly by offloading to an alternate resource.

The first step in developing bills of resources is to determine which resources to include. A few paragraphs ago, we used the phrase "key resources." That implies that not all resources are visible to Rough-Cut Capacity Planning, just the important ones. Important ones are often large resources, which could be entire departments such as Filling.

On the other hand, a key resource might be a single piece of equipment, perhaps one of a kind, which causes problems when it's overloaded. Labeler #6 (in Figures 4-3 and 4-4) might be an example of this; perhaps it's a portable labeler that can move from line to line, and is the only one that can apply a specific type of label.

Figure 4-5

ROUGH-CUT CAPACITY REPORT

Resource: FILLING

Demonstrated Capacity: 450
Maximum Demonstrated Capacity: 482
Unit of Measure: Hours

Month		1	2	3	4	5	6	7	8	9	10	11	12
Load vs. Demonstrated Capacity													
Month	Load	529	486	488	402	394	364	592	410	550	556	487	491
	Pct	1.1756	1.08	1.0844	0.8933	0.8756	0.8089	1.3156	0.9111	1.2222	1.2356	1.0822	1.0911
Cumul	Load	529	1015	1503	1905	2299	2663	3255	3665	4215	4771	5258	5749
	Pct	1.1756	1.1278	1.1133	1.0583	1.0218	0.9863	1.0333	1.0181	1.0407	1.0602	1.0622	1.0646
Demonstrated Capacity													
	Month	450	450	450	450	450	450	450	450	450	450	450	450
	Cumulative		900	1350	1800	2250	2700	3150	3600	4050	4500	4950	5400
Load vs. Maximum Demonstrated Capacity													
Month	Load	529	486	488	402	394	364	592	410	550	556	487	491
	Pct	1.0975	1.0083	1.0124	0.834	0.8174	0.7552	1.2282	0.8506	1.1411	1.1535	1.0104	1.0187
Cumul	Load	529	1015	1503	1905	2299	2663	3255	3665	4215	4771	5258	5749
	Pct	1.0975	1.0529	1.0394	0.9881	0.9539	0.9208	0.9647	0.9505	0.9716	0.9898	0.9917	0.9939
Maximum Demonstrated Capacity													
	Month	482	482	482	482	482	482	482	482	482	482	482	482
	Cumulative		964	1446	1928	2410	2892	3374	3856	4338	4820	5302	5784

Reasons to include a resource in the rough-cut process include:

• It's a bottleneck (for example, the Filling department).

• It's not possible to offload work from this resource to another (Labeler #6).

• It has a long lead time to change capacity (highly trained production people).

- It's heavily involved with new products (perhaps engineering people).

- It's costly to underutilize, such as equipment designed to run 24-7 and/or expensive to shut down and restart. Furnaces are a good example.

When a resource is shown to be overloaded, what options are open to rectify that condition? Well, there are many: use overtime, add people, add a shift, offload work to an alternate resource, subcontract, cut lot sizes, and many more. The issue is that the overload must be rectified; if not, then an imbalance exists between the demand for capacity and its supply — and such a plan is not producible.

If the supply of capacity cannot be increased, then the demand for it must be reduced and that normally happens via a reduction in the forecast. Normally this is not a good thing. These are the kinds of issues that are addressed during the monthly S&OP cycle, as we'll see in the next chapter.

The resources being addressed can, of course, be production resources but also could be others. Material, warehouse space, refrigerated storage, shipping department labor, cash, and others can be appropriate subjects for Rough-Cut Capacity Planning when they are constraints to producing and shipping product. In some of these cases, e.g., material, the driver is the Operations Plan. However, the driver for warehouse space would be the Inventory Plan and perhaps the Forecast/Sales Plan would drive the calculations for shipping labor. In Finish-to-Order, the driver for the Finishing Department would also be the Forecast/Sales Plan. Appendix F contains additional details on this topic.

Beware of including too many resources in this process. Dozens and dozens are probably too many. One good rule of thumb is to track a number of resources no more than double the number of product families, i.e., ten families, no more than 20 resources.

As with forecasting, many companies are able to do an effective job of Rough-Cut Capacity Planning at the family or subfamily level. This occurs when the families or subfamilies are fairly homogenous, i.e., when the individual items within them create a fairly similar load on the resources. Other companies find that, closer in, they need to build up the Rough-Cut Capacity Plan from the Master Schedule, because the individual products place widely differing loads on the resources. Hence, individual item detail is necessary in these cases.

In my experience, most companies don't need that kind of precision for projections many months into the future. Some companies feel they need such precision, but if you think your company may be in that category, make sure that you're not confusing precision with validity. Four-decimal-place "accuracy" isn't necessary; what's needed are valid numbers, directionally correct, upon which to base decisions.

Please see Chapter 13 for more on displaying and using rough-cut information.

The Interaction of Lean Manufacturing and S&OP

First, let's look at alignment. Lean Manufacturing leads companies to create aligned resources. One of the bedrock elements in Lean is to create flow, and very often this will result in rearranging the production facilities to line up with the products. Therefore:

- If you have already converted to Lean, you probably already have aligned resources.

- If you're converting to Lean now, try to ensure that the Lean initiative will result in aligned resources. (This will probably happen, because Lean leads to aligned resources.)

- If you've not yet started on your Lean journey, be aware that when you do, you should be able to simplify your Rough-Cut Capacity Planning dramatically because your resources will probably have become aligned. This is a typical outcome. One more time: Lean simplifies the operating environment, which enables the simplification of the forecasting, planning, and scheduling tools necessary to control it.

Although this is a chapter on inputs, I'd like to look at several potential S&OP outputs in a Lean environment. One of the key operating values in Lean is *Takt Time*, i.e., the seconds or minutes required to produce one item, sometimes called the "drumbeat" for the process. Takt Time communicates the frequency of demand, and consequently the frequency at which a product must be produced by the finishing process.

The basic calculation of Takt Time is: operating time divided by quantity required. For example, if Acme's customers require 240 items per day and the plant operates 480 minutes per day, Takt Time is 120 seconds (two minutes). To meet customer demand, sufficient resources, both in people and equipment, must be available to produce one unit every 120 seconds. The cell or finishing line for the product needs a proven output rate, *Engineered Cycle Time* in Lean parlance, which is 120 seconds or less. Key points:

• Using the language of demand and supply, we can say that Takt Time is the *demand* for capacity and that Engineered Cycle Time represents the *supply* of capacity. Supply must equal or exceed demand, or the total demand will not be met and the customers will be disappointed.

• Takt Time is the rate of production required to meet *customer* demand. This is the simplest approach, when conditions allow.

• However, there are sometimes other issues that need to be considered in setting actual production rates. Products with seasonal sales curves, plant vacation shutdowns, inventory adjustments, intermittent large demand shifts, and other factors — all of which are reflected in S&OP's Operations Plan — may require a wider view than pure Takt Time provides.

• *Operational Takt Time* is the rate of production required to meet customer demand *and* the other factors just cited. Within the context of Sales & Operations Planning, pure Takt Time would be calculated from the Sales Plan (customer orders and forecasts); Operational Takt Time would be derived from the Operations Plan, which is the pure demand plus or minus necessary adjustments.

Prior to implementing Lean Manufacturing, Company L had been successfully utilizing Sales & Operations Planning. As they transitioned to Lean, it was quite natural for them to integrate calculations for Takt Time and Operational Takt Time and a comparison to their Engineered Cycle Times into the process and make it part of the normal monthly reviews.

Since Company L's business was increasing nicely, they used S&OP as the source for calculating Takt Times and Operational Takt Times well into the future. With this, people in Operations could see future workload for months out into the future, and thus were able to determine how best to increase Engineered Cycle Times to meet the coming increases in demand.

For more on the utilization of S&OP with Lean Manufacturing, please see Appendix A, which contains a sample spreadsheet prepared by Chris Gray. He is one of the most knowledge people around on the topic of integrating S&OP with Lean Manufacturing.

Demand/Supply Strategies

It's necessary to define an operating approach for each product family, and we refer to such approaches as *demand/supply strategies*. These strategies spell out whether the product family is

Make-to-Stock, Make-to-Order, or Finish-to-Order; what the target customer service levels are; and the desired level of inventory or customer order backlog. These inventory and backlog targets are essential: along with the forecast, they drive the Operations Plan.

In Figure 4-6, we can see two examples of demand/ supply strategies. In this example, Acme Widget has said that the Medium Consumer Widget family contains primarily Make-to-Stock products, that it wants to provide 99 percent on time and complete customer service for these products, and that doing so will require ten days of finished inventory.

Figure 4-6

EXAMPLES OF DEMAND/SUPPLY STRATEGIES

Product Family: Medium Consumer Widgets

1. Make-to-Stock
2. Target Customer Service Level: 99% Line Item Fill
3. Target Finished Goods Inventory: 10 Days' Supply

Product Family: Large Industrial Widgets

1. Make-to-Order
2. Target Customer Service Level: 98% Order Fill
3. Target Customer Lead Time: 4 Weeks

Large Industrial Widgets are Make-to-Order products. As such, there is no finished goods inventory for them; rather, the variable here is the size of the customer order backlog, which directly determines the customer lead time.

Let's look at that target customer service level for Medium Widgets. It says 99 percent Line Item Fill. That means that 99 percent of all line items are to be shipped on time and complete. That sounds fine until you consider that Acme Widget averages five line items per customer order, and most orders call for items from different families. The measure that should be used to track customer service should, in almost all cases, not be line fill but rather order fill — the percentage of customer orders shipped on time and complete.

So what is Acme doing messing around with line item fill in their demand/supply strategy? The answer is: they have to. You see, the strategies are specific to a family, and they drive the forward planning logic of S&OP. But the important customer service measure is order fill. Acme recognized that. Early in each Executive S&OP meeting, they address overall customer service performance using order fill statistics. Their *order fill* target is 95 percent. In order to reach that, since they average five items per order, they set their *line fill* target at 99 percent.

Setting the targets for inventory and order backlog is, for most companies, an imprecise science. Unless you have very good data readily available, you can't get highly accurate here; don't make a career out of trying to decide what they should be. Regarding the size of the finished goods inventory, my advice is to get started in S&OP by setting the targets at roughly what you have now — unless they're obviously much too high or low. Then, as you move through time and improve your processes, you can adjust them — usually downward.

Part of the issue here involves mix — how many different line items are in a given family. Let's take two product families with identical overall volumes. Everything about these two families is the same except for one thing: Family A has 4 items and Family B has 400. Which family would require the larger safety stock to give the same level of customer service? The answer is B, of course, because the same volume spread over 100 times more items will require much more protection against stockouts.

For Make-to-Order products, the target customer lead time is largely a function of the customer order backlog, which in turn is typically a trade-off between the desire to get the product to the customers quickly and the amount of time needed for pre-production, production, and post-production activities. Here also, my general recommendation is to get started with roughly what you're doing now, and then sharpen it up as you go along.

Let's revisit this issue of Make-to-Order or Make-to-Stock. For purposes of Sales & Operations Planning, many companies who initially think they're Make-to-Order are actually Make-to-Stock. Let's take Company D as an example. They make shopping bags, among other things, for retailers. Many of their bags are customer-specific; they show the customer's name: Nordstrom, Abercrombie and Fitch, Brooks Brothers, and so on.

Sounds like Make-to-Order, right? Well, not quite. Company D has "stocking agreements" with many of its customers that require certain levels of finished goods inventory. For S&OP this is a Make-to-Stock product, not a Make-to-Order one. The question is not primarily whether the product is built for one customer only, but rather whether the product typically goes to a finished goods inventory after it's produced. If it's the latter, it's a Make-to-Stock product for our purposes.

Commercial aircraft manufacturers are largely Make-to-Order. They finish producing the plane for a given airline, take it up for a test hop, slap a green sticker on it, and away it goes. That's Make-to-Order. Company D's shopping bags, for S&OP purposes, are Make-to-Stock.

Time Zones

Many companies using S&OP have a ground rule that says, "The current month is a done deal." They mean that there's not much possibility of changing production rates *economically* within the current month. Now keep in mind, they're talking about volume. Mix is different; it's easier to change schedules close in as opposed to changing overall run rates.

Will companies using S&OP ever change volumes close in? Yes, if it's practical, if the needs of the business require it, and if the costs and other consequences of not changing exceed the those involved in making the change. But normally they'll try to avoid making close-in rate changes.

We've just seen a simple example of a time zone.[7] A slightly more complex example might be:

- Hold the current month.

- Month 2 (in the future) — changes +/– 20 percent are okay.

- Months 3 and 4 — changes +/– 30 percent are okay.

- Months 5 and 6 — changes +/– 40 percent are okay.

- Month 7 and beyond — open.

For companies needing a more formal time zone structure like these, it's a good idea to spell them out in the Sales & Operations Planning policy. See Chapter 12.

Please note: people can decide to override time zone directions. Time zones are there mainly to serve as guides for decision-making and to help avoid jerking the plant around unduly. One of the plant's jobs, I submit, is to become increasingly flexible so that it can respond *economically* to close-in changes. That makes for happy customers and happy colleagues in Sales and in Finance.

To sum up, setting demand/supply strategies means spelling out what you're trying to accomplish with each product family in terms of demand and supply. Here are some questions that play into this:

---

[7] Time zones are delineated by *time fences.* Sometimes these two terms are used interchangeably.

• Is this family Make-to-Stock, Make-to-Order, or Finish-to-Order?

• What is the target customer service level for this family? This refers to on-time and complete shipments to customers.

• If the family is Make-to-Stock, what is the target finished goods inventory level? In other words, how much inventory is needed to enable the target customer service level?

• If the family is Finish-to-Order, what is the target inventory level of modules (or other "surrogates")? Here again, how much inventory is needed to enable the target customer service level?

• If the family is Make-to-Order, what is the target customer order backlog? Remember, in the Make-to-Order world, backlog — negative inventory — is a key factor; it determines how long it will take for customers to get their product from you.

This is important. These demand/supply strategies — simple statements of goals and targets — spell out what we need to do to keep our customers happy and to effectively manage our inventories and order backlogs. They direct us in balancing demand and supply. They're necessary for S&OP because they play a key role in the logic of the spreadsheet. In addition, as we'll see in Chapter 16, they help to keep the need for continuous improvement visible as the company goes through time.

FREQUENTLY ASKED QUESTIONS

We have several pieces of equipment that are really bottlenecks. They're individual machines, not entire production departments. Can we do Rough-Cut Capacity Planning on them?

Absolutely. These individual units are resources, perhaps small in size but big in impact. For S&OP purposes (overall volume), treat them as you would any other key resource. The issue is not purely one of size, or head count, or throughput; it's whether this resource is a *shipment stopper*.

Chapter 5

The Monthly S&OP Process

The essence of Sales & Operations Planning is decision-making. For each product family, a decision is made on the basis of recent history, recommendations from middle management, and the executive team's judgment and knowledge of business conditions. The decision can be:

- change the Sales Plan,

- change the Operations Plan,

- change the inventory/backlog plan, or

- none of the above: the current plans are okay.

These decisions form the agreed-upon, authorized plans by the president, all involved vice presidents, and other members of the Executive S&OP Team. It's important that they be documented and disseminated throughout the organization. They form the overall game plan for Sales, Operations, Finance, and Product Development. (New product plans are reviewed within S&OP in terms of their impact on the demand and supply picture.) These groups break down the aggregate plans from S&OP into the necessary level of detail: individual products, customers, regions, plants, and materials.

Sales & Operations Planning, however, is not a single event that occurs in a two-hour Executive S&OP meeting each month. Rather, preliminary work begins right after month's end and continues for some days. The steps involve middle management and some others throughout the company (see Figure 5-1). They include:

- updating the Sales Forecast;

- reviewing the impact of changes on the Operations Plan, and determining whether adequate capacity and material will be available to support them;

- identifying alternatives where problems exist;

- identifying variances to the Business Plan (budget) and potential solutions;

- formulating agreed-upon recommendations for top management regarding overall changes to the plans, and identifying areas of disagreement where consensus is not possible; and

• communicating this information to top management with sufficient time for them to review it prior to the Executive S&OP meeting.

Thanks to the work that's gone before, the Executive S&OP meeting should not take a long time — two hours or less is the norm with companies that do this well. The net result of S&OP for the top management group should be less time in meetings, more productivity in their decision-making processes, and a higher quality of work life. And most of the middle-management people involved in the earlier pre-SOP processes will experience the same benefits.

Another point about timing concerns *elapsed* time: How long should it take to complete the entire cycle from start (at the beginning of the month) to finish (the Executive S&OP meeting)? The answer is about ten to twelve work days, which puts the Executive meeting in the third week of the month.

You may be thinking:. By then, the month is more than half over. Isn't that a problem? Answer: no, it's not. And the reason why it isn't gets at what the S&OP process is all about. It's not a detailed scheduling meeting; it's not a shortage meeting; it's not a meeting to decide which jobs are going to ship next Tuesday. Rather, it's a medium- to long-term planning process, focusing primarily on months two through six and the end of the fiscal year.

A further point: during implementation, companies should not worry about getting the cycle completed in a dozen work days or less. During implementation, the main objective is to get the process working, not to hit some arbitrary timing point. Take your time; do it right; don't let people burn out by doing all-nighters — and if that means you don't have the Executive meeting until the fourth week of the month, that's okay. After you get the process working well, then you can focus on pulling in the timing.

Let's take a look at each of the steps shown in Figure 5-1.

Step 1 — Data Gathering

Most of this activity occurs within the Information Systems department, and it happens shortly after the end of the month. It consists of three elements:

• Updating the files with data from the month just ended — actual sales, production, inventories, and so on.

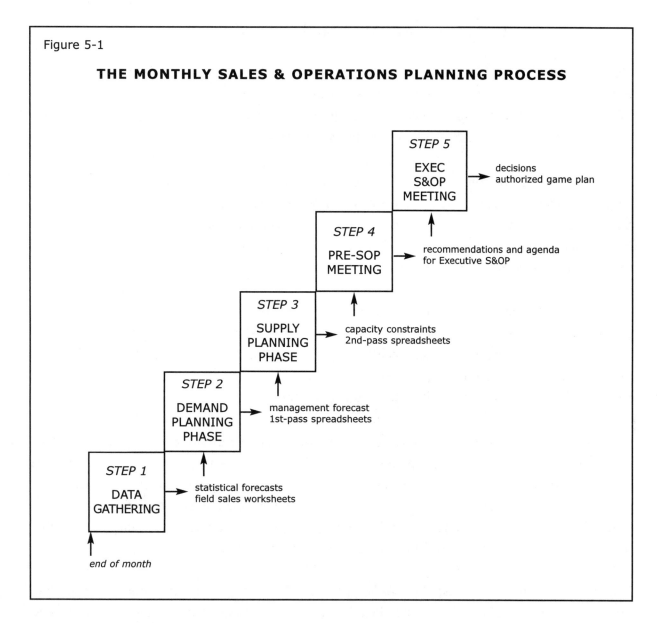

Figure 5-1

THE MONTHLY SALES & OPERATIONS PLANNING PROCESS

- Generating information for Sales and Marketing people to use in developing the new forecast. This could include sales analysis data, statistical forecast reports, and worksheets for field sales-people.

- Disseminating this information to the appropriate people.

To make S&OP a timely process overall, it's important that this step be completed within a day or two after the end of the month.

Step 2 — The Demand Planning Phase

This is where people in Sales review the information they received from Step 1, analyze and discuss it, and generate the new management forecast for the next fifteen or more months. Please keep in mind: this forecast must include both existing products *and* new products. Let's look at two very different businesses and see how the forecasting process might be carried out.

The Acme Widget Company has two divisions: Industrial and Consumer. The Industrial business is largely a Make-to-Order operation, with relatively few customers taking almost all of the volume. In this business, a very large portion of the forecasting task is customer contact: learning from the key customers their future plans for the use of Acme's products. Statistics on past sales can be helpful but the key is to capture what the customers think is going to happen.

The biggest help that good information can provide to the field salespeople in this kind of business is to show, by customer, what products they've taken in the past and to give the Sales folks an easy way to input new forecasts into the system. A good practice here is to direct the salespeople in the field to concentrate on the large customers and/or the high volume products, and not take up their valuable time with less important customers and products.

The Consumer Division, on the other hand, is almost totally a Make-to-Stock business. Its immediate customers are retailers, who sell the product to the end consumers — folks like you and I. There are many of these retail customers and, except for several mass merchandisers, no one customer makes up a large percentage of the Consumer Division's sales volume. The foundation for forecasting these products is statistical forecasting; Acme Widget has an effective statistical forecasting package that uses past history as a basis for statistical projections of future forecasts.

I hasten to add that the Consumer Division's approach to forecasting for the mass merchandisers and other large customers should look more like a Make-to-Order process than Make-to-Stock; the field salespeople must be in direct and frequent contact with their large-customer contacts regarding future needs.

Let's look at how the Demand Planning phase takes place within the Consumer Division. After the statistical forecast reports are generated, the information is reviewed by managers in the Sales and Marketing areas. Their job is to override the statistical forecasts where appropriate. When would that be appropriate? Any time that past history is not the best predictor of the future. What factors would make history not the best predictor? Well, quite a few:

- field input regarding large customers

- potential new customers

- new products

- promotion plans

- open bids

- price changes

- competitive activity

- industry dynamics

- economic conditions

- intra-company demand

- and, last but not least, a review of the forecast errors — usually by family or subfamily — from the prior month, an analysis of their causes, and determining the consequence on the new forecast.

It's the job of people in Sales and Marketing management to use their knowledge of these factors and possibly others to come up with the *management* forecast.[1] That is their responsibility. And, actually, it's also in their best interest. Most often, the management forecast proves to have a lower error rate. (Okay, it's more "accurate.") Why? Because the statistical forecast is based heavily on past history. As long as the future is going to be much like the past, then everything works. But usually it's not. Changes in the above factors can all make the future different from the past. It's the job of the *people,* using their innate intelligence and their knowledge of current conditions and the expected future outlook, to override the statistics and get the best forecast possible.

---

[1] One piece of the overall demand forecast not normally under the purview of Sales is *intra-company demand*. This is often handled by the Supply Chain group, sometimes called Logistics or Materials Management.

Once the numbers that make up the new forecast are put together, the job's not quite done. What's needed is to document the key assumptions that underlie the forecasts. This is important for several reasons. One is that, as the S&OP process goes forward, all of the participants can see the assumptions upon which the forecast is based. This may lead one or more of them to challenge the forecast, which is certainly legitimate. This gives the forecasters the opportunity to defend the specifics of their forecast rather than having to respond to a general comment, such as "it's too high."

The second benefit from documenting assumptions is that, after the period is over, it can be very instructive to review the assumptions and the results and learn, perhaps, why things didn't work out (or perhaps why they did). Learning from one's mistakes is one of the best ways to improve.

Some powerful statistical forecasting routines exist that take into account factors such as economic indicators, consumer attitude, and industry trends. If you're using one of these tools, great. However, my point here still applies: human judgment by knowledgeable people is essential.

Involving the folks in New Product Development is important here. They typically have the best handle on timing of new product launches; Sales should have already made forecasts, and their forecasts should be reviewed for possible changes. The resulting statements of new product demand must be included here so that the Supply people can make the appropriate plans. This should include new product launches currently underway plus others expected to be launched within the S&OP planning horizon.

The forecasts of future demand are best made in units and then translated into dollars, although it can be done the other way around if necessary (see Chapter 9). Regardless, it's critical that there be a dollar view of the updated forecast before it goes further. People from Finance and Accounting should be involved in this update; their participation here is very valuable.

Since the output from this Demand Planning phase is the management-authorized forecast, it's necessary to get the senior Sales and Marketing executive into the loop. In some companies, the forecasters make a brief presentation of the updated forecast to the vice president of Sales and Marketing. Bringing the senior executive into the process at this point does several things:

• It allows him or her to ask questions, challenge the numbers, challenge the assumptions, and if need be, change some of them.

• It avoids surprises at the S&OP meeting.

- It results in a truly "management-authorized forecast," one that all of the key players have bought into. They've signed off on it. This forecast, then, represents Sales' best estimate of future demand.

So how does the new forecast enter into the S&OP spreadsheets? One good way to do it is, first, to roll forecast, production, and inventory data inside the spreadsheet one month to the left, to reflect the passage of time. Then lay in the newly updated forecasts along with actual sales, production, and inventory data for the month just ended. The result is what I call the First-Pass Spreadsheets.

You now have the new forecast playing against the current Operations Plan, and the resultant planned inventory or backlog numbers will now be different. Some families will probably change very little, but others will show major differences from last month, because of last month's demand, changes to the forecast, inventory adjustments, and shifts in the backlog. This set of First-Pass Spreadsheets now goes into the Supply Planning step.

Do companies have a formal Demand Planning meeting? Some do and some don't. In general, larger companies tend to hold one or more formal meetings to get the management forecast nailed down, while frequently, smaller companies have a series of smaller, somewhat less formal face-to-face sessions.

People with the following kinds of job titles typically populate the Demand Planning Team:

Demand Manager	Customer Service Manager
Product Manager	Sales Administration Manager
Forecast Analyst	Accounting Manager
Sales Manager	New Products Coordinator
Salesperson	Supply Chain Manager
S&OP Process Owner	

Please note: these are generic job titles. They probably won't match up exactly with yours. Moreover, they are only examples; not all of them should be considered as mandatory. In most companies, there are normally about a half dozen to a dozen people involved in the demand planning/forecasting process.

Sometimes people question the need for Accounting and New Products to be represented in this activity. Well, the fact is that they're very important. Accounting expertise is needed on this team to determine the financial impact of changes to the forecast, for both sales and gross margins. New Product representation brings into the picture an essential element of overall demand: the demand for new products.

Step 3 — The Supply (Capacity) Planning Phase

The newly updated S&OP spreadsheets are the primary input to the Supply Planning phase, which is Operations' responsibility.

Their first step is to modify the Operations Plans for any families or subfamilies that need it. If little or nothing has changed from last month, then there's probably little reason to change anything this month. On the other hand, changes in the Sales Forecast, inventory levels, or the size of the customer order backlog can readily trigger a change to the Operations Plan.

The new Operations Plan must then be tested for doability. For companies with aligned resources, this can be done using the S&OP spreadsheets themselves. For nonaligned resources, Rough-Cut Capacity Planning is needed to focus on the demand/supply picture for specific resources.

Outputs from the Supply Planning step are the Second-Pass Spreadsheets, Rough-Cut Capacity reports, and a list of any supply problems that cannot be resolved or that require decisions further up the ladder. In some cases, demand (as expressed by the forecast) simply exceeds supply by too great a margin to reach; the constraints cannot be overcome within the allowable time. Sometimes these constraints are within the company's production resources; at other times constraints may exist elsewhere in the supply chain, i.e., outside suppliers.

At other times, acquiring the resources necessary to meet the demand may be feasible but will require spending that can be authorized only by top management. These are the kinds of issues that the supply folks carry into the Pre-SOP meeting.

As with Demand Planning, some companies will conduct a formal meeting for this Supply Planning step, while others find it more effective to simply work the process informally one on one.

This group is made up of people such as:

Plant Manager	Production Control Manager	Materials Manager
Accounting Manager	Purchasing Manager	New Products Coordinator
Master Scheduler	S&OP Process Owner	Distribution Manager

Most of the comments made for the Demand Planning Team apply here also:

- Not all of these job titles need to be represented in the process.

- Formal meetings are held in some companies, not in others.

- Accounting expertise is necessary to evaluate the financial impact of changes to the production plan.

- The impact of New Products on plant and supplier capacity must be done here.

- The senior operations executive might serve as a resource to authorize the output from this group.

Step 4 — The Pre-SOP Meeting

Objectives of the Pre-SOP meeting include:

- making decisions regarding the balancing of demand and supply;

- resolving problems and differences so that, where possible, a single set of recommendations can be made to the Executive S&OP meeting;

- identifying those areas where agreement cannot be reached, and determining how the situation will be presented in the Executive S&OP meeting;

- developing, where appropriate, scenarios showing alternate courses of action to solve a given problem;

- setting the agenda for the Executive S&OP meeting.

The key players in this meeting typically include several of the people from the Demand Planning phase, including someone from Product Development, Operations people from the Supply Planning step, one or more representatives from Finance, and the S&OP Process Owner (see Chapter 8).

Their job is to do a family-by-family review of the Second-Pass Spreadsheets, including subfamilies where they exist, and to make adjustments where appropriate. They also check for resource constraints, using either the product family/subfamily spreadsheets (for aligned resources) or separate capacity displays (for matrix resources). Where there are constraints, demand priorities must be established and that, of course, should be done primarily by Sales and Marketing people.

In addition, their review should look at actual performance to plan for sales, production, inventories and backlogs, and once per quarter a check on the demand/supply strategies for each family to make appropriate changes (see Chapter 16, S&OP Effectiveness Checklist).

The outputs from the Pre-SOP meeting include:

- An updated financial view of the business, including matching the latest sales call to the business plan for the total company. (This is typically done on a rolled-up, dollarized spreadsheet covering all families.)

- A recommendation for each product family, contained on the Third-Pass Spreadsheets, as to the future course of action:
  ✓ stay the course, no change;
  ✓ increase/decrease the Sales Plan; and/or
  ✓ increase/decrease the Operations Plan.

- New product launch issues not covered within the product family review.

- A recommendation for each resource requiring a major change: e.g., add people, add a shift, add equipment, offload work to a sister plant, outsource, or reduce the number of people or shifts.

- Areas where a consensus decision could not be reached, possibly as a result of disagreement or where competing alternatives might be "too close to call." In such cases, it's often very helpful for alternative scenarios to be presented — Plan A, Plan B, Plan C — with dollar data as well as units, to show the financial impact.

- Recommendations for changes to demand/supply strategies, where appropriate.

- Agenda for the S&OP meeting, an example of which is shown on the next page.

The Pre-SOP team includes folks such as:

Demand Manager	Materials Manager	Customer Service Manager
Forecast Analyst	Product Manager	Master Scheduler
Plant Manager	Purchasing Manager	Accounting Manager
Controller	New Products Coordinator	Supply Chain Manager
Logistics Manager	S&OP Process Owner	

Don't be put off by the apparent size of this group. Yes, there are eleven job titles identified here, but frequently several functions are performed by the same person.

On the other side of the coin, some job titles may contain more than one person, e.g., three product managers and two plant managers. Therefore, it's possible that you would wind up with a group that's a bit larger than what you're used to. At that point, you either drop people off the team, or get started with the larger group and see what happens.

SAMPLE AGENDA

EXECUTIVE
SALES & OPERATIONS PLANNING
MEETING

1. Macro Business Review

2. Customer Service Performance

3. New Products

4. Family-by-Family Review and Decisions

5. Production/Procurement Rate Changes

6. Collective Impact on Business Plan

7. Recap of Decisions Made

8. Critique of Meeting

I'm more comfortable with the second option. To me it's far better to have a group slightly larger than ideal than to exclude people who can contribute to the process. One factor in favor of the larger size is that these meetings are not brainstorming sessions. Rather, they're structured meetings with a high degree of focus on the process. Virtually all of the players will have already participated in one or both of the prior steps, so there won't be a large number of surprises or new issues to work through.

To sum up, the Pre-SOP meeting is in one sense a "get-ready" session for the Executive S&OP meeting. But it's actually a lot more than that: the Pre-SOP is a *decision-making* session. The mind-set that the Pre-SOP participants should have is, "If this were our business, what would we decide to do?"

Step 5 — The Executive S&OP Meeting

This is the culminating event in the monthly S&OP cycle. Its objectives are:

- To make decisions about each product family: accept the recommendation from the Pre-SOP Team or choose a different course of action.

- To authorize changes in production or procurement rates, where significant costs or other consequences are involved.

- To relate the dollarized version of the S&OP information to the Business Plan and where they deviate, decide to adjust the Sales & Operations Plan and/or the Business Plan, as appropriate.

- To "break the ties" for areas where the Pre-SOP Team was unable to reach consensus.

- To review customer service performance, new product issues, special projects, and other issues and to make the necessary decisions.

Outputs from the Executive S&OP meeting include the meeting minutes, which spell out the decisions that were made; modifications to the Business Plan, if any; and the Fourth-Pass Spreadsheets, which reflect changes made at the Executive meeting.

All these things taken collectively form the company's authorized game plan. As such, there is urgency to get the word out to all involved people, and for this reason I recommend that the meeting minutes and the Fourth-Pass Spreadsheets be distributed within two working days of the meeting.

This group should include, at a minimum, the:

    President (General Manager, COO)
    Vice Presidents of:
        Sales
        Marketing
        Operations
        Product Development
        Finance
        Logistics
        Human Resources
    S&OP Process Owner

Most Executive S&OP Teams I've been involved with are not this small. Rather, they include other people who can add value to the process, such as the Demand Manager, Product Manager, Sales Manager, Customer Service Manager, Supply Chain Manager, Plant Manager, Materials Manager, Master Scheduler, Supply Planner, Controller, and New Product Coordinator. The comments that I made for the size of the Pre-SOP team apply here also.

A company near where I live was implementing S&OP. The two plant managers were on their Pre-SOP team but were not included in the Executive S&OP meeting, in order to keep the group small. At the time, the company was facing a number of tricky capacity issues, and they found that their Executive S&OP meetings were difficult and not as productive as they could have been. They just didn't have enough plant-specific knowledge in the room to make decisions crisply.

I was serving as the company's S&OP expert. My job, therefore, was to address serious issues like this and help to get them resolved. I recommended to the president and the Vice President of Operations that the two plant managers be added to the Executive S&OP meeting team. After a bit of "arm wrestling" on the part of the VP, they did add the two plant managers, and things went a lot better from then on.

Here's a quick point for those of you in smaller companies. You may not need to have both a Pre-SOP meeting and an Executive S&OP meeting. In some companies or business units, perhaps around $30 million or less per year, the line between operating managers and executives gets blurred. The operating-level managers report directly to the president. I've seen some companies in this category combine the Pre-SOP and Executive S&OP meetings into one — and it's worked well. What is called for, in that case, is a president with a fair amount of patience, because there's no Pre-SOP session to get all the ducks in a row.

Tips for Effective Executive S&OP Meetings

Over time your meetings should become very effective. Here are some ideas to help you achieve that.

- **Send out the agenda in advance.** Getting the agenda out several days before the meeting gives the participants a chance to see what decisions they'll be asked to make.

- **Include the important S&OP spreadsheets with the agenda.** This will give the participants a chance to review the status of the major product families and resources.

- **Use a projector at the meeting.** This focuses the group's attention, keeps everyone on the same page, and helps people to better understand the pros and cons of the decisions they're making.

- **Have enough Pre-SOP people at the Executive S&OP meeting to answer likely questions.** Having to scramble to get information or to reconvene the meeting later represents inefficient use of the Executive Team's time.

- **Have a preappointed minute-taker.** This person should be someone other than the facilitators or presenters.

- **Be time-efficient.** If necessary, designate a time-keeper to keep the meeting moving.

- **At the end of each meeting, take five minutes to review the decisions made.** This ensures that all of the decision-makers heard the same thing and understand the decisions coming out of the meeting.

- **At the end of the meeting, take five minutes to critique the process.** Each participant should be asked for comments. This step speaks to continuous improvement and helps to ensure that the meetings get better and better. Initially this should be done at every meeting; later, once the process is working well, every second or third month should be sufficient.

- **Distribute the minutes within two work days of the meeting.** This meeting sets the company game plan for the upcoming months, so there should be a sense of urgency to get the word out as to what those plans are.

FREQUENTLY ASKED QUESTIONS

What if there's a major event — affecting demand and supply — that occurs shortly after the Executive S&OP meeting? It doesn't make sense to wait another whole month to address such a big issue.

It certainly doesn't. Many successful S&OP users, when confronted with such situations, will use an abbreviated, accelerated S&OP process. They'll go through the Pre-SOP steps very quickly, focusing only on those parts of the business that are affected. Then, within a day or two, they'll conduct another Executive S&OP session and make the necessary decisions.

Throughout the abbreviated process, they try to keep the steps, the report formats, and the decision-making process the same — because the people are familiar with those processes and know they're solid.

Part Two

How to Make It Work

Chapter 6

The S&OP Implementation Path Overview

Would you agree that what you've seen so far is fairly simple? No open heart surgery, no orbital dynamics, no advanced calculus. But there's a paradox here: even though this process itself is very straightforward and easy to understand, it is *difficult* to implement it successfully. Here's why:

- It's a new process for the company.

- New processes mean change.

- Change, in this context, means people changing some aspects of how they do their jobs.

- People need a solid understanding of the process and a vision of the future in order to willingly and enthusiastically make the necessary changes.

- Top management people are usually very busy and thus have a low tolerance for spending time on unproductive activities. Progress must be made quickly and consistently. If that doesn't happen, the implementation project may stall out and never reach a successful conclusion.

So it's hard to do this right. The good news is that, when you implement it, you don't need to reinvent the wheel. There is a proven implementation path, developed over the years by trial and error. If you do it correctly, you can have near-100 percent assurance that your implementation of S&OP will be successful.

Please take a moment and look at Figure 6-1. It contains the generalized S&OP Implementation Path, which shows a number of tasks to be completed, some sequentially and some in parallel. It indicates that the time required for a complete implementation will be about nine months for the average organization. Here also, there's a bit of a paradox. Why does something that involves relatively few people take eight or ten months to implement? It's because of the nature of the S&OP process. It occurs on a monthly cycle. During implementation, incremental experience and expertise are gained only once each month.

For almost all of the companies implementing S&OP that I've observed over the years, benefits come sooner than six months. The reason lies in S&OP's ability to provide that window into the future mentioned in Chapter 1. Take another look at Figure 6-1.

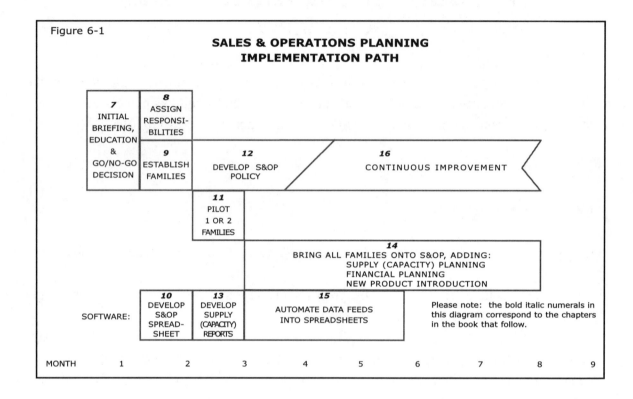

Figure 6-1

Check the third row down — Pilot 1 or 2 Families — and the fourth row — Bring All Families Onto S&OP. Almost invariably, in about month two or three, people are able to see things that they wouldn't have without S&OP. It's common to hear comments like, "Golly. If we weren't doing this, we'd have had a big problem with Medium Widgets. We'd have got slammed about four months from now." Being able to get a better focus on the future means that problems can be avoided by taking early corrective action.

There's more to the S&OP Implementation Path than a diagram. In Appendix B, you'll find a verbal version of the Implementation Path diagram. It is a generalized outline for companies to use to tailor their own project schedule for implementation. Developing a solid project schedule will, I'm convinced, get you through the project sooner and with a greater probability of success.

Therefore, as soon as possible after steps 7 and 8, develop your detailed project schedule and get concurrence from all of the key players.

To recap, two important things to keep in mind regarding S&OP implementation:

- Even though the logic of S&OP is simple, implementing it is not. Implementing it requires people to make changes — to do some aspects of their jobs differently — up to and including the senior executive in charge of the business.

- Because of the monthly cycle, it will take about eight months to implement the basics of Sales & Operations Planning. Benefits, however, will start to be realized much sooner.

In the chapters that follow, we'll discuss each of the boxes in the Implementation Path diagram shown in Figure 6-1. Please note that the individual boxes in the diagram are coded to the chapters that follow.

Chapter 7

Executive Briefing, Education, and Go/No-Go Decision

Virtually all business processes center around people, and S&OP is certainly no exception. My colleagues and I have been saying for years that people are the A item, as in ABC — Pareto's Law. The B item is data, and the computer is the C. Very simply, people are by far the most important element in Sales & Operations Planning, and thus the people part of the project must be done very well.

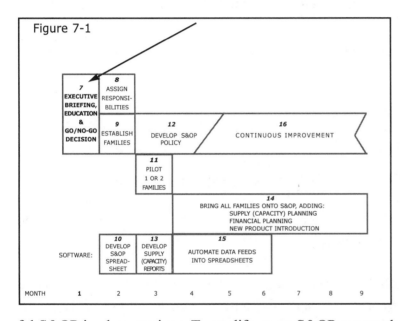

Figure 7-1

The S&OP Expert

In the pages that follow, I'm going to recommend to you that you involve an *S&OP expert* in your implementation of S&OP — for the initial executive briefing, for the education sessions to follow, and for periodic status and progress checks during the implementation.

An S&OP expert is someone who's been deeply involved in at least one — preferably multiple — successful S&OP implementations. To qualify as an S&OP expert, the individual needs to have been in a significant leadership role in directing the implementation. You may have an S&OP expert working in your company, for example, if he or she has successful and meaningful S&OP experience at, say, a sister division or another company.

A good example concerns a guy named John. John was the COO at a company where I was in the role of S&OP expert. John served as the executive champion, and the company soon became very successful with S&OP. John subsequently left that company and became the CEO at a somewhat smaller firm. There, he very successfully filled the role of S&OP expert. He could do this because he had "been there." He had experienced how to make it work.

Most often, however, such a person will not be on board. Thus you'll need to obtain your S&OP expert from among the ranks of consultants active in this field, most of whom are in the supply chain and resource planning fields. They are not rookies; they have many years of experience not only in operating jobs but also as consultants, and they are totally comfortable in communicating with top management.

When you're talking to someone regarding your S&OP executive briefing, education sessions, or other S&OP support, I recommend strongly that you check his or her references. You need positive answers to the following kinds of questions:

- Have you been involved in one or more implementations of Sales & Operations Planning?

- How successful were those implementations?

- What were your roles in those implementations?

- Where were those implementations, and can I talk directly to the companies?

- Do you have a process, a methodology for implementing S&OP?

If the answers to all these questions are positive, and if the companies being referenced confirm them, you should be in good shape. If not, look elsewhere.

Some of you might be thinking, "What's the big deal? This S&OP stuff is simple." Sure it is, the basic logic and process — as we said at the start of Chapter 6. Thus, it's easy to get blindsided by the simplicity of S&OP's logic. Don't make the mistake of thinking that because it's not structurally complicated, it'll be easy to make it work. It won't.

Peter Tassi, with the Ford Motor Company's Lean Manufacturing Center, says it superbly: "The soft stuff is the hard stuff." Implementing S&OP successfully is mostly about dealing with people issues. The role of the S&OP expert is to help keep those people issues from becoming people problems and thus derailing the project.

Let's examine those potential people problems, which can be split into two categories: individual and organizational. Individual people problems include:

- aversion to change,

- a schedule that is too busy — or is perceived as such,

• reluctance to share information and control.

And, of course, there are others. In the organizational category, here are the three problems I've seen most often:

• discomfort with accountability. Some organizations have difficulty with accountability; it makes them nervous. But S&OP puts a spotlight on accountability.

• aversion to conflict. Some organizations don't like to deal with conflict. However, S&OP often *forces* conflict to be addressed.

• lack of discipline and self-discipline. In some companies, the prevailing mind-set is to do one's own thing. If that means not preparing for meetings, or not showing up for them . . . well, the corporate culture says that's okay. However, S&OP is a cross-functional, highly interdependent, team-based process. The members of the team must be able to be counted on to do their part.

Most companies can expect to encounter some of these kinds of problems, both individual and organizational. Most often they need experienced, skilled help and facilitation to work through them. Bottom line: most successful implementations have involved an S&OP expert in a major way.

Executive Briefing — Making the Business Case

For most companies, the best way to get started with S&OP is to conduct an initial briefing — at the executive level. This is a several hour session facilitated by the S&OP expert.

The purpose of the executive briefing is to transfer enough information about the process to enable the senior management group to:

• Understand the capabilities of Sales & Operations Planning. They need to learn what it does, how it works (in very general terms), and what kinds of benefits companies have realized from using it.

• Match S&OP's capabilities to their business problems. This is where the business case is made for Sales & Operations Planning. What problems is the company experiencing in shipping to its customers on time, running the plants effectively, keeping finished goods inventories low and customer order backlogs in line? Which of these would get better if S&OP were used well?

- Learn how S&OP is different from current practices, even if the current process is already called S&OP.

- Develop a rough-cut benefit statement, covering both hard benefits (financial) and soft ones: enhanced teamwork, better decision making, more control over the business.

- Understand how the process is implemented and what will be required of the company in general, and the executive group in particular.

- Make an informed decision, if possible, to implement S&OP.

Please note the two words: *if possible.* Most often it's possible to do so; in some cases, however, people need to learn more about S&OP before they're comfortable making this type of go/no-go decision. In these cases, the decision should be to go to the next step, the education sessions.

One last point. In some companies, it's possible to skip the initial briefing and go right to the education step, because the go/no-go decision has already been made. This could be the case where some key people have already learned a bit about S&OP at a seminar, or where the president has prior S&OP experience and is convinced of its merits, or where there's been enough informal talking and reading about S&OP that the senior management group is comfortable with the concept and has committed to it. But while it's okay to skip the initial briefing, it's *not* okay to skip the next step: education.

The Education Sessions

There are two main reasons for taking time to learn about Sales & Operations Planning. One is to enable people to learn more about this process so that they can make a solid commitment to implementing it, if they haven't already done so. Second, an education session establishes a common framework, viewpoint, and terminology for the people who will be involved in operating Sales & Operations Planning.

This step, led by the S&OP expert, should involve all of the people who will be "hands on" with S&OP — top management, middle management, and others, e.g., forecast analysts, salespeople, planners, and schedulers.

The primary objective of these education sessions is for the people to gain that solid understanding of the S&OP process and to see the compelling business reasons for it — in order to willingly and enthusiastically make the necessary changes, including some aspects of how they do their jobs.

This is as true with top management as with any other group in the company, because they're so deeply involved with decision making. Making the right decisions today is tougher than ever because of the rapid pace of change. As we said earlier, better processes yield better results; better decision-making processes yield better decisions. And that's what much of the top management job is all about: making better decisions — more productively, on a more timely basis, and with higher quality — than the competition's executives.

Executives and everyone else to be involved need to understand that S&OP is a superior decision-making process. Therefore it's a very important tool for both top and middle management, and thus those folks need to learn about it.

My colleague, Bob Stahl, has developed a superb method for education. He divides it into three phases, with each successive phase involving fewer people and more detail:

First Half-Day

Topic: Basics of S&OP: what it is, where it fits, how it works, how it's different from today's practices, what benefits result, how it's implemented.

Attendees: Everyone who will be "hands-on" with S&OP plus other interested people. This definitely includes Top Management. If Top Management isn't present, the people in the session will probably be saying: "This S&OP stuff sounds good, but *they'll* never do it." *They*, of course, refers to top management.

Emphasis: How S&OP can benefit the company and how to implement it successfully.

Second Half-Day

Topic: How to apply S&OP practices to the company.

Attendees: Most of the people who were present in the first session, except for top management. It's really not necessary that they be present for this part, although they should feel welcome to stick around if they wish. One exception to this is the Executive

Champion or Sponsor, the person with executive responsibility to oversee and support the implementation effort. (For details, please see the next chapter.) If he or she has already been identified, then by all means that person should be present in the afternoon session. If not, then one or several members of the executive group should be present to provide a top management presence and viewpoint.

Emphasis: How S&OP will work here in the company.

Third Half-Day

Topic: Development of a detailed implementation plan.

Attendees: The people who will be hands on with S&OP, less the executive group but including the Executive Champion.

Emphasis: The creation of a detailed implementation plan with tasks, responsibilities, critical paths, timing, and resource requirements — concluding with a live pilot within 90 days.

It's not necessary to have these sessions separated by one or more days. Usually, the first two half-days occur on the same day, followed by the third half-day the next morning.

So, who do you get to present and facilitate these sessions? The S&OP expert, of course, whom we mentioned in the prior section. If that person did a good job at the executive briefing, then he or she is the logical person to lead the education sessions.

Go/No-Go Decision

Often this event occurs before the education sessions. One example, as we saw earlier, is that of a newly hired president who used S&OP successfully at his or her prior company and wants to bring it into the new organization. Decision made. Or, the president and other key members of the Executive Team learn about S&OP, perhaps at a public seminar, and become convinced that they need to do it. Decision made. Or maybe the decision gets made in conjunction with the Executive Briefing.

In other cases, the decision has not yet been made — or at least ratified. In this situation, following the education sessions, I recommend that the Executive Team plus other involved people get together and make a formal go/no-go decision on S&OP. If the decision is no, for whatever reason, then the case is closed. Let's go do something else.

Most of the time the answer is yes, let's do it. I believe the main reason is that the inherent logic of S&OP is valid and compelling; for most top management people, it exerts a strong pull. I can remember the CEO of a consumer packaged goods company, upon learning about S&OP at the education session, saying, "If we'd had this 25 years ago, I'd be a younger man. I'd have fewer scars — and more hair."

FREQUENTLY ASKED QUESTIONS

In our company, we're doing much of S&OP but without top management. We've tried to get them to have an initial briefing with no luck. They won't read the books or even the articles. What should we do?

What you should *not* do is give up. Try to keep your S&OP process going through all of the Pre-SOP steps. Where practical, start to display your S&OP spreadsheets in meetings with top management. Try to present recommendations within the framework of the S&OP display. Use the same format to present alternative scenarios to support difficult decisions.

Further, try to enlist an Executive Champion and work with him or her to move the process upward in the company. Your Executive Champion might be successful in getting a standing time slot, say twenty or thirty minutes, once a month at an executive staff meeting. Use this to recap the Pre-SOP meeting. After this has been happening for a few months, start asking the executive group to ratify the decisions made in the Pre-SOP.

Steps like these and possibly others might pay off in the long run. And the downside risk seems to be almost nonexistent.

Chapter 8

Assign Responsibilities

Once the decision is made to proceed, it's time to get the project organized. Here's what needs to be addressed in terms of roles and responsibilities.

Executive Champion/Sponsor

It's important to have one executive assigned to champion the S&OP project. He or she can be a big help in keeping executive attention focused on the project, removing impediments, acquiring needed resources, and supporting the S&OP Process Owner and the other folks doing the heavy lifting. He or she should be willing to provide leadership, spend some time, and carry the flag for S&OP.

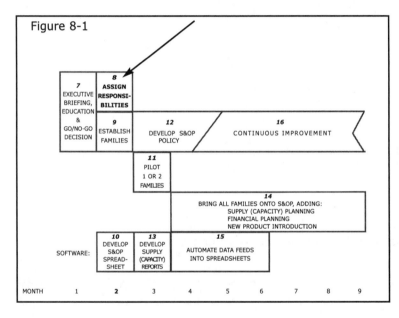

Figure 8-1

Who should it be? In general, my first choice would be the president — provided he or she has the time and the inclination. If not the president, then take your pick from any one of the VPs. Ideally, the person selected would be enthusiastic about Sales & Operations Planning and would have a solid working relationship with the president. Of far less importance is whether their current assignment is in Sales, Operations, Finance or wherever.

S&OP Process Owner

There needs to be a process owner, someone who will lead the implementation project and, most often, continue in a process leadership/ownership role over time. This is normally not a full-time job. You won't need to free someone up from all other duties to do this.

So what should this person look like and from where in the organization should he or she come? I don't believe it should be a top management person (primarily for reasons of time availability) but it should be someone with solid managerial experience. The person should have good people skills, be proactive and well organized, and be able to lead a meeting effectively. He or she should know the business — the people, the products, the processes, and last but definitely not least, the customers. Do not fill this role with an outside hire; it will take an outsider a long time to learn these critically important elements of your business.

Okay, so where should the S&OP Process Owner come from: Operations, Sales, Marketing, Purchasing, Finance? My answer is here also, take your pick, with one caveat: it's best if the Process Owner and the Executive Champion come from different departments. This avoids sending an unintended message that this project is a "Sales and Marketing deal" or an "Operations deal" or whatever.

S&OP Process Owners I have known include:

- Director of Sales Administration

- Demand Manager

- Supply Chain Manager

- Materials Manager

- Controller

- Sales Manager and Materials Manager (a joint, shared assignment).

At Company A, Ken had been on board for about eight years and was the Production Control Manager at their largest plant (one of four). Ken is a self-starter, and before S&OP came onto the company's radar screen, he had already started doing some S&OP-like planning for his plant. When the company decided to go with a formal Sales & Operations Planning process, he was tapped to head up the project and the process. He moved from the plant to the corporate office, became responsible not only for S&OP but also for forecasting, and now reports to the vice president of Sales.

Company R's general office was in Connecticut with its manufacturing headquarters located in Kentucky. There were dual S&OP Process Owners, one for each location. At the general office, the Director of Sales Administration led the effort, while the Process Owner at the manufacturing headquarters was the Director of Materials Management. They were in frequent contact and shared meeting facilitation responsibilities at both the Pre-SOP and Executive S&OP meetings.

One of the first jobs for the S&OP Process Owner and Executive Champion should be to address the implementation project schedule as discussed in Chapter 6. A process that works well is to:

1. Prepare a tentative, rough draft of the schedule.

2. Circulate the draft to all involved people.

3. Get their feedback and make the appropriate changes.

4. Publish the schedule.

5. Track progress against the schedule.

6. Report on the project's status at each Pre-SOP and Executive S&OP meeting.

Spreadsheet Developer

You might find this curious — to include what may seem to be a rather mundane function. Perhaps, but I learned the hard way not to overlook it. In Chapter 10, we'll get into the spreadsheet topic in depth, but for now let's just say that the odds are very high that your S&OP information will be displayed by spreadsheet software (such as Excel or one of its worthy competitors). Setting them up will be somewhat complex. But that's not all.

During the first six months of implementing S&OP, you will probably change your spreadsheets at least four or five times. The changes won't usually be major, but they will require some time and effort. I've found it helpful to have one person designated as the developer and maintainer of the spreadsheet.

An interesting possibility: if your S&OP Process Owner is reasonably good with spreadsheets then perhaps he or she could handle this task.

Populate the Teams

This refers to the important step of assigning people to the various teams: Demand Planning, Supply Planning, Pre-SOP, and Executive. In Chapter 5 we showed a suggested composition of each of these groups, and you may want to refer to that now.

Support from the S&OP Expert

Here's some more good news: unlike some other initiatives, with S&OP you won't need to have an army of outsiders — systems integrators, junior consultants, or whatever — swarming all over your company. On the other hand, as we said earlier, support from an S&OP expert can be a big help in making this process work. This expert's role is to teach, to encourage, to head off problems before they occur, to help solve problems that have occurred, to keep the project on the rails, to push — hard, if necessary — for visible progress each and every month so that the project doesn't stall out. Remember, we said earlier that this is a people project. The soft stuff is the hard stuff.

Not an enormous amount of the expert's time should be required to do that. For a typical company, an average of one to two days per month for about eight months has proven to be adequate — with more days being applied early in the process and fewer later. If the expert is an outsider, make him or her part of the team. Keep your expert in the loop. Don't hesitate to talk to that person frequently on the phone.

Among companies that have used this kind of outside expertise, the percentage of successful implementations is very high. Among companies that haven't done so, the success rate is much lower.

FREQUENTLY ASKED QUESTIONS

What about setting up an S&OP project team or task force? Can this be helpful?

It may be. In larger companies, where the operating environment tends to be more complex, this can be quite helpful. For a business of average size and complexity, I've not found it to be necessary. What needs to be managed and accomplished can typically be handled well by the Executive Sponsor and the S&OP Process Owner working with the Demand, Supply, Pre-SOP, and Executive S&OP teams themselves.

****

Does everyone have to sit through the entire meeting (Pre-SOP or Exec), or can people come and go as needed?

For me this question is more relevant for the Pre-SOP meeting, which can be lengthy. I've seen it work well for the folks from, say, Plant A to be in the first part of the meeting, followed by the Plant B people. But please note: if Plants A and B make some of the same products and have similar resources, this approach might not work. When workload needs to be reassigned, you really need both groups in the room at the same time.

Product managers might need to stay only as long as their products are being discussed — provided also that there's no significant interrelationship or capacity conflicts between their products and those of some other product manager. The same goes for New Product Development. The Finance representative would probably be there for the entire session, as would the Demand Manager, Materials Manager, S&OP Process Owner, and others.

I don't think this question is germane for the Executive S&OP meeting. That session lasts no more than two hours, and it's this meeting that gives overall direction to the business. Two hours or less seems to me to be a very good investment of people's time. Even in those parts of the meeting when they're not directly involved, they'll still be getting good input on the overall status of the business.

Chapter 9

Establish Families, Subfamilies, and Resources

Here are some of the issues to keep in mind when setting up your product families and resources.

Families — How Many?

If you have more than about a dozen product families, you probably have too many. Why? Well, it gets down to the mission of S&OP: it's a decision-making process for top management to use in balancing demand and supply.

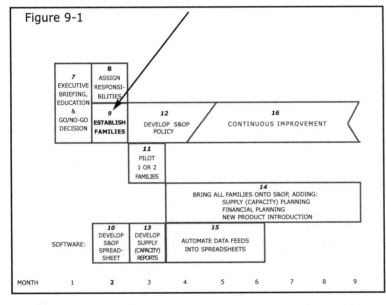

Figure 9-1

Having worked with numerous top management teams over the years, I can assure you of several of their characteristics: first, they're very busy; second, they therefore have limited attention spans; and third, they are therefore not interested in getting into lots of detail unless it's absolutely necessary. Having to review twenty or thirty or more product families once each month does not fit that profile.

Thus, if you have too many families, top management will tune out. If top management tunes out, the process will die. Hands-on, active participation by top management is essential for this decision-making process to be effective.

The best number of product families is around six to twelve. When you start to get much above that, you're probably asking for trouble.

Families — How to Select Them

Many companies, prior to getting into S&OP, have their product families effectively identified. In their budgeting and business planning processes, the families are spelled out, and they make perfectly good sense. If you're in that category, great. Use what you have for S&OP.

In other companies, they haven't yet spelled out a good product family array and doing that is an important early step. Among the options here are to structure your product families by:

- product type (scotch, bourbon, gin)

- product characteristics (high performance, de luxe, standard)

- product size (large, medium, small)

- brand (Accord, Civic, CRV, Pilot, Odyssey)

- market segment (industrial, consumer)

- distribution channel (mass merchandisers, original equipment manufacturers, aftermarket)

- customer.

The fundamental question is, simply, how do you go to the marketplace? Acme Widget's products, for example, fall logically into Industrial and Consumer, and then into subdivisions — small, medium, and large — within those two.

Companies with Make-to-Order products will sometimes set up their families by customer, with perhaps the 20 percent of customers who account for 80 percent of the business spelled out as individual families and the remaining low-volume customers grouped into one family.

Making Use of Subfamilies

How, you may be thinking, is it possible to define a complex business in just a few families? My question for you is: what is your purpose? If you're talking about filling customer orders and making shipments, you need to work with individual products and customer orders. However, you can't do Sales & Operations Planning at that level even if you wanted to, because S&OP is a tool for *aggregate* planning. Its focus is on *volume,* not mix.

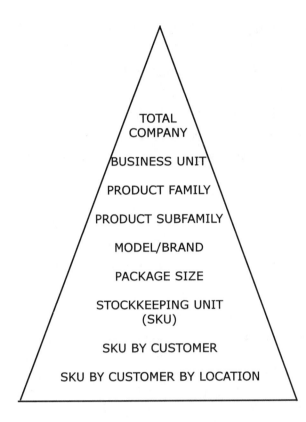

TOTAL
COMPANY

BUSINESS UNIT

PRODUCT FAMILY

PRODUCT SUBFAMILY

MODEL/BRAND

PACKAGE SIZE

STOCKKEEPING UNIT
(SKU)

SKU BY CUSTOMER

SKU BY CUSTOMER BY LOCATION

In Chapter 4, we discussed at which level to forecast, and we identified the possibilities shown at the left. Obviously we can't do S&OP at the very top of the pyramid, because there's not enough granularity at that level upon which to base demand/supply decisions.

Toward the bottom of the pyramid, there's too much detail; we're flying fifty feet off the ground at 400 knots. We're surely not going to see the big picture down there. There's an area in this pyramid that sits below the high-level product families used in the Executive S&OP meeting and above individual products, and we refer to these intermediate groupings as "subfamilies."

For example, the Acme Widget Company, as we saw, has two product lines — Industrial and Consumer. Within each category, there are three product families: small, medium, and large. The Consumer product line has a further subdivision: seasonal and everyday. Acme people often need to view these separately; the seasonal line requires extensive early production prior to the onset of the peak Christmas selling season, while demand and production for everyday products is, of course, more stable. When planning the pre-build, with its attendant rise in inventory, top management people want to see the plan so they can approve it. They also want to view it during the height of the season. However, during most of the year, it's not of interest to them *unless something is going wrong.*

It's the job of the Pre-SOP Team to monitor the subfamilies to ensure that they're performing to plan. When they're not, the Pre-SOP people need to fix them, and sometimes that requires a decision (e.g., for reasons of cost, impact on other parts of the business, or staffing levels) from top management. In such cases, the Pre-SOP Team is empowered to elevate a subfamily, along with their recommendation, to the Executive S&OP meeting for a decision. This has the dual advantages of keeping the top management folks in the loop when needed, but not taking up their time unnecessarily.

Product Families and Nonaligned Resources

Products are what the company provides to its customers, and a company's families should be organized on that principle. Set up your families based on what makes sense to the folks in Sales and Marketing. Make sure the families line up with market segments, customer groups, or, when appropriate, individual large customers. When you do that, you'll probably find that your families *do not line up with your resources* — plants, departments, and processes. That's because most companies don't have aligned resources.

That's okay. Don't make the mistake of trying to force-fit the resource picture into your product families. The result is usually a mish-mash that doesn't do a good job. Rather, identify your non-aligned resources separately and view their status by means of the Rough-Cut Capacity Planning process we talked about in Chapter 4.

Unit of Measure

When setting up your product families, it's necessary to specify the unit of measure to be used for each family. Choices for unit of measure include but are not limited to:

each	cases	thousands	pounds
tons	gallons	liters	kilos

For most companies, selecting the units of measure is a no-brainer. On the other hand, some companies really struggle over this issue. Here also, the point about separating demand and supply applies: pick the units of measure based on how you go to the marketplace. Then, if Operations needs something different, derive that with Rough-Cut Capacity Planning.

FREQUENTLY ASKED QUESTIONS

How about using dollars as the primary unit of measure?

Only as a last resort. Certainly we need to see dollars because the financial view is essential for running a business well. But it's far easier to go from *units to dollars* than the reverse. So the message is: plan in units and translate to dollars.

There are, however, times when it's just not possible to use units. One company I worked with, making process control computers, had product families with processors, monitors, modems, readers, power supplies, and on and on. There was simply no common unit of measure that spanned all the diverse products within a given family. Therefore, they used dollars because they had no choice. And it worked well.

****

Does it ever make sense to have the product families based on how Operations views things?

Only if that arrangement also works for Sales. If so, what you probably have are aligned resources. If that arrangement doesn't seem to work well for Sales, then the key questions include:

• Will it be more difficult for Sales to do a good job of forecasting?

• Will it be more difficult for Sales to relate the S&OP process to how they go to market and how they work with customers?

If the answer to either of these is yes, it will be more difficult for Sales, then I recommend against doing it.

Chapter 10

Develop S&OP Spreadsheet

We had a preliminary look at several S&OP spreadsheets in Chapter 3. Now it's time to get into the details and understand how they work. We'll get started with the sample spreadsheet in Figure 10-2 on the following page.

Make-to-Stock and Finish-to-Order Format

In Figure 10-2, for a Make-to-Stock product family called Medium Widgets, the demand/supply strategy specifies a target customer service level (shipments on time and complete) of 99 percent. The target finished inventory necessary to support this shipping performance has been set at 10 days'

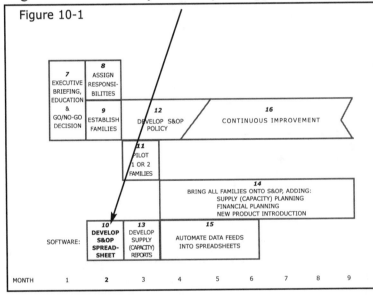

Figure 10-1

supply, (work days, not calendar days). See the area in Figure 10-2 identified by *A.* Let's examine the 10-day inventory target. Why does this company feel it needs 10 days of finished goods inventory? The answer is that its experience over the recent past has shown that 10 days is a minimum level necessary to provide 99 percent customer service.

Should this 10-day supply target be considered a constant, fixed far out into the future? Not at all. The

principle of continuous improvement should drive this company to improve its sales, production, and logistics processes so that 99 percent customer service becomes attainable with only, say, 9 days of supply. And then 8 days. And then 7. But for now, the realities of life are that it takes about a half month's worth of inventory to provide the 99 percent service level.

In *B,* actual sales are compared to forecast. For the past three months, sales are running ahead of forecast by 44,000 units. Actual production performance to the plan is evaluated in *C.* It's close to being perfect.

Area *D* shows inventory performance to plan, and the actual customer service performance. We can see a serious problem developing here: as the forecast was oversold, the actual inventory went below plan. The result is that customer service has dropped to 89 percent for September, quite a bit below its 99 percent target.

Figure 10-2

THE ACME WIDGET COMPANY — SALES & OPERATIONS PLAN FOR OCT 2004

FAMILY:	MEDIUM WIDGETS (MAKE-TO-STOCK)	**A**	UNIT OF MEASURE:	1000 UNITS
TARGET LINE FILL:	99%		TARGET FINISHED INV:	10 DAYS ON HAND

B / **E**

SALES	HISTORY J	A	S	O	N	D	J	F	M	3rd 3 MOS	4th 3 MOS	12 MO TOTAL	MOS 13-18	FISCAL YR LATEST CALL	BUS PLAN
OLD FORECAST	200	200	200	200	200	200	200	200	200	660	660	2520	1320		
NEW FORECAST				210	210	220	220	220	220		690	2670	1470	$25,540M	$25,400M
NEW VS. OLD FCST				10	10	20	20	20	20	30	30	150	150		
ACTUAL SALES	222	195	227												
DIFF: MONTH	22	-5	27												
CUM		17	44												

C / **F**

OPERATIONS	J	A	S	O	N	D	J	F	M	3rd 3 MOS	4th 3 MOS	12 MO TOTAL	MOS 13-18
OLD PLAN	200	200	200	210	210	200	200	200	220	660	660	2540	1320
NEW PLAN				210	220	230	230	230	230	690	690		
NEW VS. OLD PLAN					10	30	30	30	10	30	30		
ACTUAL	200	206	199										
DIFF: MONTH	0	6	-1										
CUM		6	5										

D / **G**

INVENTORY	J	A	S	O	N	D	J	F	M	3rd	4th	12 MO
PLAN	100	100	100	61	71	81	91	101	111	111	111	
ACTUAL	78	89	61									
DAYS ON HAND	8	9	6	6	6	7	8	9	10	10	9	
LINE FILL %	97%	98%	89%									

DEMAND ISSUES AND ASSUMPTIONS **H**

1. FORECAST REFLECTS LAUNCH OF NEW DESIGNER WIDGET LINE IN 3RD QTR.
2. ASIA FORECASTED TO REACH 2001 VOLUME

SUPPLY ISSUES **I**

1. XMAS FULL PLANT SHUTDOWN RESCHEDULED TO STAGGERED PARTIALS THRU FALL AND WINTER

The new Sales Forecast is shown in *E*. Towards the right of the page you'll find a total for the next rolling twelve months, as well as totals in units and dollars for the fiscal year, ending in December in this example.

As a result, the fiscal totals are made up of both sales history (Jan.–Sept.) and Sales Forecast (Oct.–Dec.). Farther to the right is the forecasted dollar amount in the Business Plan. This latter number allows for an easy comparison between the Business Plan and the S&OP forecast for the fiscal year's volume. On the basis of this, the top management team will probably elect to change the Business Plan accordingly.

Also in *E,* please note that the old forecast is shown in addition to the new forecast. Many companies like to do this so they can see the magnitude of the changes. The same approach is being taken in the Production section, comparing the old plan with the new

The assumptions that underlie the forecast are listed in area *H,* in the lower left-hand corner. The future Operations Plan, based on the new forecast and other considerations, is shown in *F,* and the relevant supply (production/procurement) issues are listed in *I.*

Area *G* contains the future inventory projection for finished goods, both in units and days-on-hand. The unit calculation is:

Last month's ending inventory (e.g., end of September: 60)

minus

This month's new Sales Forecast (October: 210)

plus

This month's new Operations Plan (October: 210)

equals

This month's ending inventory (October: 60)

The projected days-on-hand calculation is:

Next month's new forecast (e.g., November: 210)

divided by

Number of work days in month

(We're using a straight 20 days per month in this spreadsheet.

In Chapter 13, we'll see a spreadsheet with varying work days per month)

equals

Daily sales rate (210/20 = 10.5)

divided into

This month's inventory plan (October: 60)

equals

This month's days' supply (October: 5.7, rounded to 6)[1]

---

[1] In prior months, actual inventory is used rather than plan. In our example, July's actual was 78, August 89, September 61, yielding the days' supply numbers of 8, 9, and 6, respectively.

In summary, Figure 10-2 is an example of a proven, effective format for Sales & Operations Planning. The intent is to have all of the relevant information for a given product family on one display. That enables each family's situation to be viewed completely and organically, both its recent past performance and its future outlook. For decision-making purposes, this has proven to be far superior to individual displays of information that focus only on sales, or on inventory levels, or on production.

The Finish-to-Order format looks like the one for Make-to-Stock, except that it deals with "module inventory" or some other kind of surrogate inventory as opposed to finished goods.

A caution: as you get started, try not to let the spreadsheet get too "busy." It's easy to keep adding this piece of data and then that piece, until the display gets very crowded and hard to read. Keep it simple, at least in the beginning. There'll be plenty of time to add things later.

Make-to-Order Format

A spreadsheet for a purely Make-to-Order family isn't treated much differently from Make-to-Stock (see Figure 10-3). As we saw in Chapter 3, the main difference is that the spreadsheet for Make-to-Order doesn't contain data for finished goods inventory. That's because there is none. (If there were, then the family wouldn't be purely Make-to-Order.) Rather, the inventory numbers are replaced by a display of the customer order backlog — both past and projected.

The other difference is that, in projecting the backlog into the future, the calculations are reversed from Make-to-Stock. In Make-to-Order, demand is added to the projected backlog and production is subtracted from it. (In Make-to-Stock, demand is subtracted from the projected inventory, and production is added to it.)

Here's how the projected backlog calculation works:

Last month's ending backlog (e.g., end of September: 30)

plus

This month's new bookings forecast (October: 20)

minus

This month's new operations plan (October: 20)

equals

This month's ending backlog (October: 30)

Figure 10-3   THE ACME WIDGET COMPANY — SALES & OPERATIONS PLAN FOR OCT 2004

FAMILY: LARGE WIDGETS (MAKE-TO-ORDER)   UNIT OF MEASURE: EACH

TARGET LINE FILL: 99%   TARGET ORDER BACKLOG: 4 WEEKS

| | | H I S T O R Y | | | | | | | | 3rd | 4th | 12 MO | MOS | FISCAL YR | BUS |
BOOKINGS	J	A	S	O	N	D	J	F	M	3 MOS	3 MOS	TOTAL	13-18	LATEST CALL	PLAN
OLD FORECAST	20	20	20	20	20	20	20	20	20	60	60	240	120	$1,800M	$1,800M
NEW FORECAST				20	20	20	22	24	24	72	72	274	142	$2,055M	$1,800M
NEW VS. OLD FCST				0	0	0	2	4	4	12	12	38	22	$255M	
ACTUAL BOOKINGS	22	20	21	20	20	20	8								
DIFF: MONTH	2	0	1												
CUM		2	3												

PRODUCTION/SHIPMENTS															
OLD PLAN	20	20	20	20	20	20	20	20	20	60	60	240	120		
NEW PLAN				20	21	22	24	24	24	72	77	284	142		
NEW VS. OLD PLAN				0	1	2	4	4	4	12	17				
ACTUAL	20	21	20												
DIFF: MONTH	0	1	0												
CUM		1	1												

ORDER BACKLOG															
OLD PLAN		30	30	30	30	30	30	30	30	30	30				
NEW PLAN				30	29	27	25	25	25	25	20				
ACTUAL	28	30	29	30											
BACKLOG — # WEEKS				6	6	5	5	5	5	5	4				
ORDER FILL %		99%	100%	100%											

10% TIME FENCE

DEMAND ISSUES AND ASSUMPTIONS

1. FORECAST REFLECTS INCREASED SALES
   BECAUSE OF PROBLEMS AT COMPETITOR
   PLUS SORTER LEAD TIMES

SUPPLY ISSUES

1. UNABLE TO REACH 4 WEEKS BACKLOG UNTIL AUGUST BECAUSE OF:
   A) FORECAST INCREASE, AND
   B) NEW EQUIPMENT NEEDED TO GO BEYOND 24 UNITS PER MONTH
      NOT AVAILABLE UNTIL JULY

I used a simplified calculation for the number of weeks of backlog, as follows:

New (production/shipment) plan (e.g., November: 21)

divided by 4 (weeks in a month) equals

Weekly plan (5)

divided into

Ending backlog (October: 30)

equals

Backlog in weeks (October: 6)

Here again, with both Make-to-Order and Make-to-Stock, my advice is to keep the spreadsheet as uncluttered as possible.

One last point regarding the Make-to-Order spreadsheet: in this example, we're showing a time fence at the end of the third month into the future. It's labeled "10% time fence," which means that production rate changes within the first 90-day zone should be held to 10 percent or less. As with all time fences, it should be considered as a guideline only and not a hard and fast rule. Typically it will mean that overriding the time fence carries significant costs or other penalties, so a decision to change it should be made thoughtfully and by the right people.

Graphical Displays

Traditionally in S&OP, product family spreadsheets had been displayed in tabular form, i.e., numbers. On the other hand, Rough-Cut Capacity information seems to lend itself better to graphs, and so we've seen more of those over the years.

However, many people have preferences for graphs over tables, and we're starting to see more companies displaying their S&OP product family spreadsheets in graphical form. Graphs are less efficient in their use of space, but are easier to understand. A sample graph is shown in Figure 10-4 for a Finish-to-Order family, but of course graphical displays could be used equally well for Make-to-Stock or Make-to-Order families.

The display is divided into three sections: *Performance*, which contains recent history; *Plan*, the outlook for sales, operations, and inventory out through the 18-month planning horizon; and *$ Projection*, containing the financial outlook focusing on the end of the fiscal year. This last section seems to work better with numbers rather than graphs, so it's been kept in tabular form.

Please consider this sample as just that — something to stimulate your thought processes. This display is limited by the lack of color, which forces the graphs to be shown separately rather than on a combined basis. That's one opportunity for improvement and I'm sure there are others.

The Spreadsheet Checklist

As you design your spreadsheets, you might want to keep the following checklist handy. It contains the ten items that I feel are essential for an effective spreadsheet:

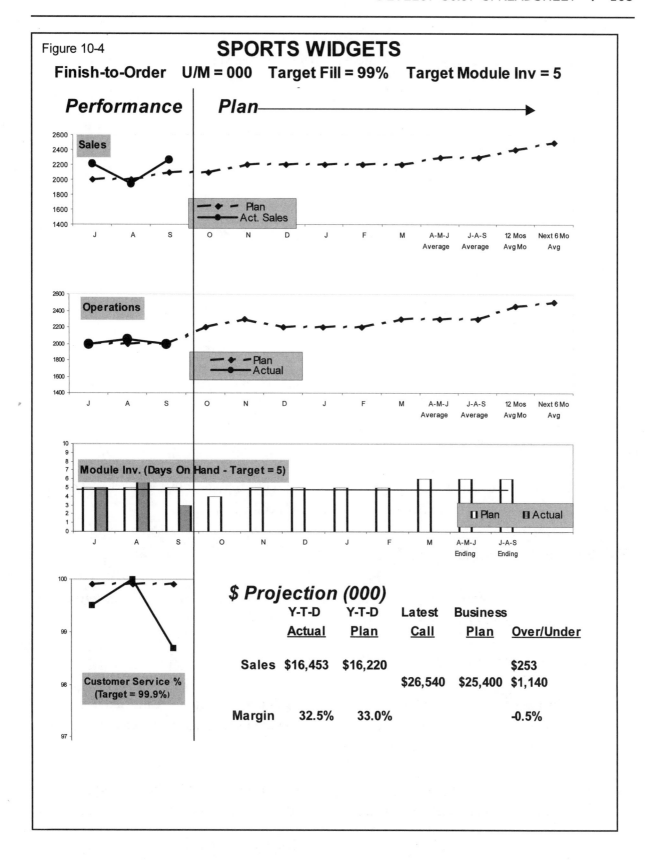

Figure 10-4

SPORTS WIDGETS

Finish-to-Order   U/M = 000   Target Fill = 99%   Target Module Inv = 5

- Order Fulfillment Strategy (Make-to-Stock, Finish-to-Order, Make-to-Order, etc.)

- Unit of measure

- Customer Service target

- Inventory target

- Sales actuals and forecast

- Operations actuals and plan

- Inventory or backlog actuals and plan

- Customer Service actuals

- Financial comparison to Business Plan

- Demand and Supply issues and assumptions

Insuring that you include all of these on your spreadsheet will get you off to a good start. Then add other items that will be helpful in dealing with your own specific situations.

FREQUENTLY ASKED QUESTIONS

Why does the spreadsheet need to project so far out into the future? What benefit is a forecast for fifteen months or eighteen months out?

One reason is Financial Planning, and there are two pieces to it:

- We need at least twelve months of forward "planning horizon," to compare the S&OP plan with the Business Plan for the current fiscal year. Early in the fiscal year, we'll need forecasts that "reach" to the year's end in order to do that.

- Further, we're going to begin work on next year's budget about three to six months prior to the start of the next fiscal year. At that point, we'll need the three to six months of forecast for the current year, plus twelve months for next year. Having this forward forecasting and planning information in the ongoing business planning process makes the entire budgeting cycle much less time-consuming and, dare I say, less painful. One CEO I worked with said that one of their major goals for S&OP was to free people from having to spend large amounts of time in budgeting, so they could focus on the important stuff: serving the customers, developing new products, and running the plants more flexibly and effectively. That works for me.

Another reason for a long planning horizon, of course, is for Operations people to get some feel for what their capacity needs will be down the road. If each month they're looking at a potential bottleneck out in the future, they will be able to start to think about it, kick around some ideas, and check out some possibilities *in advance of* having to make decisions. A pilot friend of mine said once that S&OP helps to "get your head out of the cockpit" so you can look out longer range.

****

Isn't it confusing to display so much information on one page?

It can be, if the display is not well designed. It's a balancing act between showing the necessary information and not showing unnecessary elements. I suggest you start off with a mind-set that "less is more." Include only the information you feel is necessary; then you can add the "nice-to's" as you go along.

However, please don't exclude the basic demand information (forecasts, etc.), the basic supply information (operations plan), and the projected inventory balance (or projected backlog for Make-to-Order). These are essential. The projected inventory or backlog represents the *critique* of the demand/supply balance, and that's what S&OP is all about.

****

Is it really necessary to use the spreadsheets in the Executive S&OP meeting? And, if so, is it necessary to view all the spreadsheets in that meeting, or could we just look at the families where something has changed and a decision is needed?

I believe it is necessary to use the spreadsheets. They're the heart of the entire process: it's on that document that all of the major demand and supply issues come together and can be viewed holistically.

For the first year or so, I recommend that you look at all of the spreadsheets, one per family. Then, after you're really proficient at the process and you'd like to speed things up, you might try it on an exception basis. But keep an open mind — you may decide it's better to cover them all.

On several occasions, I've seen an Executive S&OP group be presented with a family spreadsheet where no changes were recommended. However, looking at the spreadsheet sparked a comment and then another comment and another. This resulted in an excellent discussion regarding a previously unidentified opportunity, which became a follow-up item for further analysis and action.

Chapter 11

Pilot One or Two Families

Thus far in our S&OP implementation journey we've learned about Sales & Operations Planning, assigned responsibilities, set up the product families, and developed a first draft of the spreadsheet. Now it's time to get started on the actual process itself, and before we launch right into it, we need to ask ourselves a few questions.

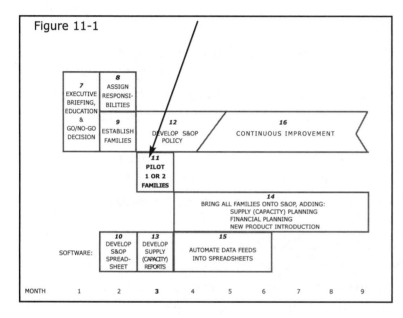

Figure 11-1

First, what's the best way to do this? Broadly, we have two choices: start up using all fam-ilies, or pilot one or two families. The title of this chapter tells you which one I prefer. The reason I prefer the pilot approach is that trying to do more than one or two families will very likely be overwhelming. It's much easier to focus on only one or two families.

Having said that, we can now examine the two main reasons for the live pilot:

- It's an essential step towards full implementation. We must get the first one or two families onto the process before we can add them all.

- There's an important element of *learning* involved with the pilot.

Let's stay with that second point, learning. The education you've had so far has been largely conceptual; the pilot starts the "on-the-job" training. The folks in the Demand Planning and Supply Planning phases learn by doing. Ditto for the Pre-SOP team.

By the time the Executive S&OP meeting rolls around, most of the people involved with S&OP have had both conceptual education and on-the-job training — except for the top management team. They're the only people who haven't yet experienced how this stuff works in their company. Plus most of them, except for the Executive Champion, haven't been as close to S&OP thus far as many others.

Therefore, the pilot Executive S&OP meeting is as much about learning as about making decisions. In this session, the Executive Champion, the S&OP Process Owner, the S&OP Expert, and others should explain how the steps of the process have been done:

• Data Gathering,

• Demand Planning,

• Supply Planning, including Rough-Cut Capacity Planning if necessary, and

• the Pre-SOP meeting, including the discoveries — "aha's" — made in that meeting. This reinforces one of the important aspects of the business case for S&OP: a window into the future.

Part of this meeting should be devoted to identifying changes in roles necessary for the process to work really well. Lastly, the top management folks should be encouraged not only to ask questions but also to provide feedback for design improvements to the displays and the process.

So, which family should you pick for the pilot, the hardest one or the easiest?[1] Here I opt for the middle of the road. Don't pick the most complicated or trickiest product family, because you might have a really tough time getting it off the ground. If your production resources are matrix rather than aligned, I suggest you avoid a family with capacity problems. Keep in mind that the main missions in this early stage are not to get operational results but rather to learn more, to implement the process, and to get it working. On the other hand, I'd be reluctant to pick a simple family that represents, say, less than 2 percent of the total business. It just doesn't have enough impact to get people excited.

I suggest you look at the three or four product families that are most important to the company. The importance could be based on sales dollars, margin contribution, or impact on customers. Within those three or four families, pick one that's not highly complex. Further, if possible, avoid families with new product introductions taking place; new products can be difficult and thus can make things complicated.

Finally, is one product family enough? After all, the title of this section references "one or two" product families. Why would you want more than one to get started? Well, think back to the Acme Widget Company. They have two business units: Industrial and Consumer. The two units have very

---

[1] The decision we're addressing here — which family or families to pilot — should actually be made earlier, when the project schedule is first developed. By that time, following the Education step (covered in Chapter 7), people should know enough to make a solid decision on the pilot.

different products; they sell into very different markets; they have separate marketing and sales staffs; and their forecasting processes are quite different. Piloting only one family, say Medium Consumer Widgets, would mean that the folks in Industrial would not have much involvement with S&OP for the entire month. In this case, I'd suggest to Acme that they pick two families: one from Consumer and one from Industrial.

Once you've selected the pilots and accomplished the tasks in the earlier steps, it's time to just do it. What's needed here is to simply follow the steps in the monthly S&OP process, which is diagramed below.

1. Data Gathering. First, run the reports and worksheets that you use to update the Sales Forecasts, and get them to Sales so they can get started on the Demand Planning phase.

In addition, get the numbers for actual sales, production, and either inventory or customer order backlog. You'll need them for the last three months if you use the spreadsheet format recommended in this book. Ideally, you can also pick up a fiscal year-to-date number for actual sales and production.

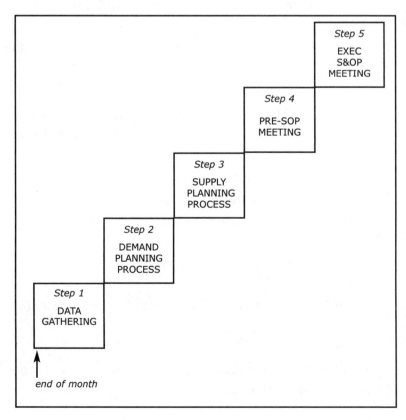

Enter the data into the spreadsheet. Down the road this data-entry function must be automated because of the volume. However, for now, most companies will enter the data manually if there will be any delay at all waiting for the feeds to be automated.

At the same time, the data must be entered for the demand/supply strategies: target customer service levels, target inventories for both Make-to-Stock and Finish-to-Order products, and target customer order backlogs for Make-to-Order.

2. Demand Planning Process. While this is going on, the Demand Planning phase can kick in. Sales generates forecasts and demand plans for the pilot family. The are entered into the S&OP spreadsheet, which then goes to Operations.

3. Supply Planning Process. Here Operations lays in the Operations Plan for the pilot family. This is set to meet the Sales Forecast and to get the inventories or backlogs to their target level. Also, Operations needs to verify that the Operations Plan is "doable" or, if not, how much of it can be achieved and determine the options to provide the rest of the needed product.

4. Pre-SOP Meeting. This is where the two groups formulate their recommendations to the Executive Team, discuss any data problems that need to be fixed, and set the agenda for the Executive S&OP meeting.

5. Executive S&OP Meeting. Here decisions regarding the pilot family are made, feedback is solicited from the group for improvement, minutes are distributed, and so on.

That's it. You've just completed your first S&OP cycle and, if you did your homework and followed the path outlined in this book, the odds are good that it was reasonably effective. It started your company down the learning curve, and you positioned yourselves for a better, easier cycle next month — when you'll be adding more families.

A caveat: don't try to get the material for the first Executive S&OP meeting to a point of perfection. Rather, in preliminary conversations with the Executive Team, the level of expectations should be set along these lines:

- *This is the first step in the implementation process. It won't be perfect and may not even be highly polished. Be patient. It will get better in a hurry. I guarantee it.*

- *We don't have all the data we need — but we have enough to get started.*

- *We're working to get all the data, but it'll take a bit longer and we didn't want to delay the implementation by waiting for it.*

Who's the best person to carry this message to the Executive Team? The Executive Champion, who of course is a member of that group. These are some of the most important things he or she can do:

• Set the level of expectations,

• Keep S&OP on the front burner with high visibility, and

• Run interference for the Pre-SOP people and others regarding such things as resource allocation.

My experience with top management groups is that they tend to be quite understanding of start-up problems and will be supportive. What they won't be happy about is seeing the same problems month after month. Making consistent progress over time is far more important than the level of polish of the first Executive S&OP meeting. It should be good, but doesn't have to be great.

Chapter 12

Develop S&OP Policy

Lots of people feel the same way about rules and regulations as I do: I'm not wild about 'em. Having said that, I hasten to add that a formal Sales & Operations Planning Policy is necessary for the successful implementation and operation of the process. It doesn't have to be anything fancy, and with luck, it will fit on one piece of paper. (Twist my arm and I'll agree to two pages, but absolutely no more.) This document should spell out the following:

- The objectives of the company's Sales & Operations Planning process

- The steps in the process

- The participants in each step of the process

- Actions to be taken at each step

I recommend that this document be signed by the president and others as appropriate.

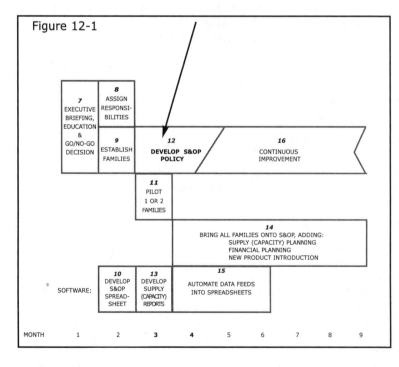

Figure 12-1

On the next page is an example of an S&OP policy patterned after one developed by a company I'm familiar with. Please note: This company held formal meetings in its Demand Planning and Supply Planning phases. They were dispersed geographically and thus had to have prearranged meeting times so that all participants could be there, either in person or by conference call. As we said earlier, some companies don't find it necessary to have formal meetings in these early steps; rather, they work the process in individual face-to-face or telephone sessions.

ACME WIDGET COMPANY — SALES & OPERATIONS PLANNING POLICY

Sales & Operations Planning establishes the overall level of sales and manufacturing output, expressed in families, to form the company game plan. Its primary purpose is to establish rates of activity that will achieve the company's objectives, including: meeting customer service and revenue goals, raising or lowering inventories and customer order backlogs, maintaining a stable work force, and enhancing the effectiveness of new product introductions.

1. The Executive S&OP meeting is held monthly in conjunction with the scheduled Officers' meeting. Attendees:

President/CEO	VP Marketing	VP Product Development
VP Finance/CFO	VP Operations	VP Sales
At least two members of the Pre-SOP Team		

Actions include: resolution of open issues from Pre-SOP, authorization or modification of Pre-SOP plans, changes to the Business Plan, New Product issues, and others as appropriate.

2. The Pre-SOP meeting is held monthly on the third Friday following the fiscal month's close. Attendees:

Controller	Logistics Manager	Product Development Managers
Customer Service Manager	Master Schedulers	Product Managers
Demand Manager/Analyst	Plant Managers	Sales Administration Manager

Actions include: development of plans to ensure a balance of demand and supply, formulation of recommendations for Executive S&OP, development of agenda for Executive S&OP, review of long-term capacity constraints, and obsolescence issues. Considerations will include: customer service levels, market strategies, inventory goals, current forecasts and backlogs, new product strategies, financial plans, current status, and capacities.

3. The Supply Planning meeting is held on the third Wednesday following the close of the fiscal month. Attendees:

Capacity Planner	Demand Manager	Plant Managers
Controller	Master Scheduler	Purchasing Manager

Actions include: review of Capacity Planning information resulting from the new forecast, review of material availability and lead time problems, manpower planning issues, cost absorption issues arising from production rate changes, and problems with new product introductions and obsolescence.

Any critical resource — manpower, equipment, supplier — whose required capacity varies from its demonstrated capacity by more than +/– 5% must be reviewed for action and possible discussion at the Pre-SOP meeting.

4. The Demand Planning Meeting is held on the second Friday following the close of the fiscal month. Attendees:

Controller	Distribution Planners	Product Managers
Customer Service Manager	Logistics Manager	Sales Administration Manager
Demand Manager/Analyst		

Actions include: approval of a forward 24-month unit and dollar forecast, review of product family trends, new product introduction issues, and special product and customer demands.

Mid-cycle djustments to the demand and supply plans can be made as required, by following the above steps on a tightly compressed schedule.

Authorized:

_____	_____	_____	_____	_____
President	Vice President	Vice President	Vice President	Vice President

Revision #: _____   Effective Date: _____

Chapter 13

Develop Supply (Capacity) Reports

This section applies mainly to companies whose production resources are organized on a matrix basis. If you have aligned resources, you won't need separate capacity reports. How so? Well, since all of the output from a given resource (department, plant, supplier) goes to only one product family, then the spreadsheet for that family can display all that department needs to know about the future workload for that resource.

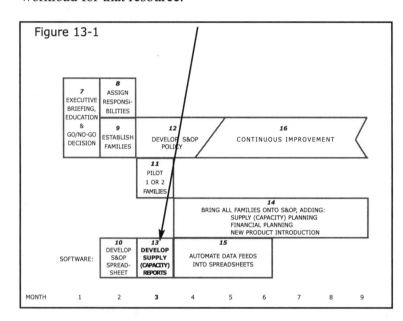

Figure 13-1

Look at the spreadsheet for Company A shown in Figure 13-2 for an example. You can see that, in the section labeled "Operations," there are rows for:

• production days per month

• daily production rate (required to hit the plan)

• Operations Plan (Line 1 times Line 2).

Their focus in the Supply Planning phase is to verify that they can hit the daily rates their plan is calling for. When they say "yes," that means they're making a commitment to hit that plan. That commitment will be noted in the Executive S&OP meeting.

I happened to attend the Executive S&OP meeting where this spreadsheet was addressed. The planned production numbers showed a sizeable increase in output. The president pressed the vice president of Operations and the Plant Manager: "Are you guys sure you can get 43,000 per day?" The answer came back: "Yes sir. You can count on it." But there's more to it than just making a commitment. Operations' commitment and all others are reviewed at the following month's meeting, when actual results are compared against plan. This is serious stuff.

Companies with matrix resources don't have it quite so easy. They will need to use the Rough-Cut Capacity Planning tool that we saw in Chapter 4. Figure 13-3 shows a Rough-Cut Capacity report from Company F, a foundry, whose products are all Make-to-Order and are sold primarily to machinery manufacturers. The resource in question is a primary manufacturing department that makes products from a wide variety of different product families.

Figure 13-2

COMPANY A — SALES & OPERATIONS PLAN FOR MARCH

FAMILY:	XRS (MAKE-TO-STOCK)												UNIT OF MEASURE:	1000 UNITS	

TARGET LINE FILL: 99%   TARGET FINISHED INV: **10 DAYS ON HAND**

	HISTORY									3rd	4th	12 MO	MOS	FISCAL YR	BUSINESS
SALES	D	J	F	M	A	M	J	J	A	3 MOS	3 MOS	TOTAL	13-18	LATEST CALL	PLAN
NEW FORECAST	750	725	724	978	802	784	939	825	811	2584	2446	10169	5200	$27,240,918	$21,411,776
ACTUAL SALES	714	794	762												
DIFF: MONTH	-36	69	38												
CUM		33	71												

OPERATIONS															
PRODN DAYS/MO	21	20	20	25	19	19	24	20	20	62	62				
DAILY PRODN RATE	32.3	39.7	41.1	43.0	41.0	40.5	40.5	40.5	41.0	40.7	40.5				
OPERATIONS PLAN	614	794	800	1075	779	770	972	810	820	2530	2511	10267			
ACTUAL	679	794	822												
DIFF: MONTH	65	0	22												
CUM		65	87												

INVENTORY															
PLAN		307	337	284	433	410	396	429	414	423	369	434			
ACTUAL	302	267	267	327											
DAYS ON HAND		7	7	9	10	10	10	10	10	10	9	11			
LINE FILL %		72%	88%	91%											

In Figure 3-3, the squares represent the *supply* of capacity: the department's demonstrated capacity at 240 hours per month, below which they don't want to drop for reasons of efficiency. The dots are based on capacity at 300 hours per month, above which they don't want to go for any extended time for reasons of employee burn-out, safety, and quality. The vertical bars represent the future workload from the Operations Plans, translated into hours, and aggregated into one number for each month. In this example, the workload is falling between the 240- and 300-hour limits for the next few months and then rises and stays above 300.

Please note: the bars — the statement of future workload — do *not* come directly from the Sales Forecast. They come from the Operations Plan, which can vary from the Sales Forecast because of backlog changes, plant shutdown, preseason production, and so on.

The decision made at the June Executive S&OP meeting was to begin interviewing for new production people in July (during plant shutdown), bring them in during August, and train them during August and September, with the goal that they'd be fully qualified and productive by October.

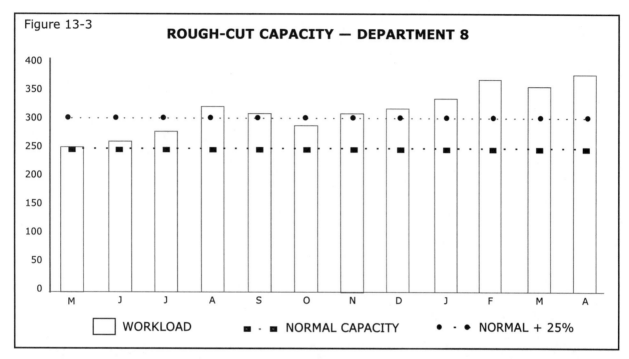

Figure 13-3
ROUGH-CUT CAPACITY — DEPARTMENT 8

WORKLOAD   ■ · ■ NORMAL CAPACITY   ● · ● NORMAL + 25%

Try to keep your Supply Planning process simple, uncluttered, and free of a lot of detail. Remember, we're dealing with aggregate volumes here for major groupings of resources. We're not trying to do finite capacity loading on each machine on the plant floor, or to develop short-term schedules. Obviously, if you have a critical piece of equipment or some other resource that is typically a bottleneck, you have to keep that clearly in view for S&OP, and the best way to do that is usually with Rough-Cut Capacity Planning.

Chapter 14

Bring All Families onto S&OP,
Adding Supply Planning, Financial Planning,
and New Products

Once you've successfully done one or two families in the S&OP pilot, it's time to start adding the other families to the process. Also, you'll be adding functions — Supply Planning, Financial Planning, and new product introductions. This time period, months four through months seven to nine, is the heart of the S&OP implementation process. It's when all of the pieces of Sales & Operations Planning come together.

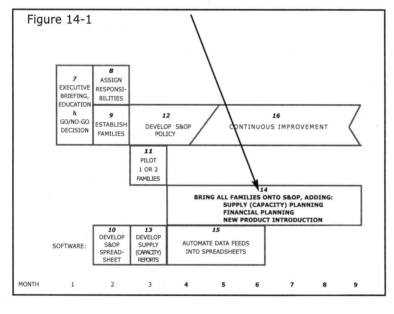

Figure 14-1

Assuming you have more than just a few families, it's best to do this in several groups of two to four families at a time, rather than to add them all at once. Adding the remaining families, say six or nine or a dozen, all at once represents an amount of work, a level of intensity, and opportunities for error that are just not worth it.

Company S had eleven product families. They piloted with one family, added three in the second month, three in the third month and four in the fourth. Along the way, as they were adding these families, they were able to:

• Dramatically improve the process.

• Clean up their spreadsheet format.

• Add Supply (Capacity) Planning.

• Add Financial Planning.

• Add planning for New Products.

• Tie the detail to the summary.

• Automate the data feeds into their spreadsheets.

Before you start this phase, decide which families you're going to cut-over onto S&OP in which months. Then add that detailed cut-over sequence into your overall project schedule.

Add Supply (Capacity) Planning

If you're an aligned company, one where the resources match up very closely with the product families, then you're adding the Supply Planning process as you bring up the various product families. As we saw in Chapter 13, you can display the capacity picture right on the S&OP spreadsheets.

If, however, you're like many companies and you have a matrix relationship between families and resources, then there's a bit of a tricky timing element here. Here's the rub: S&OP can't help you evaluate the workload on a given resource until you have S&OP planning on all of the product families serviced by that resource.

For example, Company S had a matrix arrangement regarding product families and resources. In their pilot, they weren't able to do much rigorous capacity evaluation because the pilot family was made in departments that serviced other families. (This is why I said earlier that it's best to pick a pilot family that generally hasn't been having capacity problems.) However, during the next month, they added three product families that took all of the output from two of their major production departments. At that point, they were able to start up the Supply Planning part of the process because they had a full picture of the future production requirements for those departments. And, of course, as other families were added, they got an increasingly complete picture of the overall supply side of their business and were able to do a first-rate job of identifying capacity bottlenecks early enough to take corrective action.

So if you're a company with matrix resources, set your cut-over schedule for product families with an eye towards the supply side. Bring the families onto S&OP in a sequence that enables Rough-Cut Capacity Planning to work sooner rather than later.

Add Financial Planning

The first steps here involve merely dollarizing some of the unit data on the spreadsheet — typically the rolling 15–18 months forecast and the sales projection for the current fiscal year. It's also very helpful to show the Business Plan's dollar number for that family. In that way, the S&OP number (latest call for the fiscal year, i.e., fiscal year-to-date actuals plus forecast for the balance of the year) can be readily compared with the Business Plan number for that family. Some companies show a percentage — S&OP's fiscal year projection versus the Business Plan — and that can be very helpful in quickly identifying where the big problems are. An example is shown in Figure 14-2.

Figure 14-2   DOLLARIZED SALES & OPERATIONS PLAN — OCTOBER 2004

FAMILY: **SMALL CONSUMER WIDGETS** (MAKE TO STOCK)   UNIT OF MEASURE: $000

TARGET CUSTOMER SERVICE: 98%   TARGET FINISHED INV: **10 DAYS ON HAND**

AVERAGE SELLING PRICE: $10.00   UNIT COST OF GOODS SOLD: $5.00

SALES (SALES $)	A-M-J	J	A	S	O	N	D	J	F	M	3rd 3 MOS	4th 3 MOS	12 MO TOTAL	MOS 13-18	FISCAL YR LATEST CALL	BUS PLAN
NEW FORECAST	$5400	$2000	$2000	$2000	$2100	$2100	$2200	$2200	$2200	$2200	$6900	$6900	$26,800	$14,400	$25,590	$23,000
ACTUAL SALES	6150	2200	1950	2270											+11.3%	
DIFF: MONTH		220	-50	270												
CUM	750	970	920	1190									Y-T-D MARGIN %: 32.7%			33.0%
													Y-T-D MARGIN $: $8,368			$7,590

OPERATIONS (COST)

	A-M-J	J	A	S	O	N	D	J	F	M	3rd 3 MOS	4th 3 MOS	12 MO TOTAL	MOS 13-18
NEW PLAN	$2850	$1000	$1000	$1000	$1050	$1050	$1100	$1100	$1115	$1115	$3450	$3450	$13650	$7200
ACTUAL	2610	1000	1030	990										
DIFF: MONTH		0	30	-10										
CUM	-240	-240	-210	-220										

FINISHED GOODS INVENTORY (COST)

	A-M-J	J	A	S	O	N	D	J	F	M	3rd 3 MOS	4th 3 MOS
PLAN	$450	$500	$500	$500	$300	$350	$400	$450	$500	$550	$575	$575
ACTUAL		78	89	60								
DAYS ON HAND		8	9	6	6	6	7	8	9	10	10	9
CUSTOMER SERVICE		94%	96%	89%								

DEMAND ISSUES AND ASSUMPTIONS

1. POSSIBLE ACQUISITION OF BIG MART BUSINESS NOT INCLUDED IN THIS FORECAST

SUPPLY ISSUES

1. NEW EQUIPMENT AT MIDDLETOWN PLANT TO BE INSTALLED THIS MONTH

Actually, it's possible to get a start at this during the pilot phase. However, since it's usually quite a push to get that first pilot family's unit numbers put together, most companies wait until the following month to get started on the dollars.

The dollarized sales forecast is normally expressed in average selling price. Care should be taken here. The average selling price should be periodically verified to ensure that issues such as new products, changes in the level of promotions, price and discount changes, and so forth are reflected.

Dollarized production and inventory data is expressed in cost dollars and it's usually not a big challenge to assemble that information. Adding actual gross margin data for the year-to-date can be helpful and should be easy to get, but projections of margins into the future are subject to the average selling price issue cited earlier.

An important step in the overall financial integration is to aggregate all the dollarized product family information into one view of the entire business, a sort of "master spreadsheet." Obviously, this can't be done completely until all of the families are on S&OP. And even then you might not have it all because of other revenue streams that are outside the array of product families. One approach in such cases that's proven helpful is to create a "Miscellaneous Family," to serve as a collector for atypical streams of income. Other companies just disregard this kind of thing and compare the total sales projection (out of S&OP) with a business plan number adjusted to exclude the miscellaneous incomes.

The total company dollar aggregation — the master spreadsheet — serves another purpose over and beyond sales and margin projections. For companies with Make-to-Stock families, it projects the planned levels of finished goods inventory for the total business. This can be valuable in companies whose business is highly seasonal. Frequently such companies engage in preseason production with a corresponding build-up in finished inventories. The inventory dollars can get quite large. They can represent a significant cash commitment that should be planned for well in advance. With S&OP operating in dollar mode, this kind of information is always available on the master spreadsheet, updated each month to reflect changing conditions.

Once the master spreadsheet is available, it can be used in a somewhat similar fashion as the product family spreadsheets, particularly as regards performance to plan. Actual financial results can be compared with the plan for those periods. Projected sales and margin dollars can be compared with the Business Plan and appropriate corrective action decided upon.

And this leads us to one of the key issues regarding S&OP and running the business. Sometimes S&OP's latest fiscal year call — actual YTD plus forecast, in dollars — does not match the Business Plan within a few percent. In that case, what should be done? Well, you could do nothing and change neither plan. Or you might change the Sales & Operations Plan, change the Business Plan, or change them both. Let's look at each option, starting with the first one mentioned.

Change neither. I recommend against this. To leave these two very important plans with a gap between them results in running the business with two sets of numbers: the Sales & Operations Plan is directing our ongoing activities — what we buy, what we make, what we sell — down one path;

while the Business Plan — representing our commitment to the corporate office, the board of directors, and so forth — is saying something else.

This can create confusion, lack of control, a diminishing of the perceived importance of both plans, and a greater risk of not hitting the Business Plan. Not good.

Change the Sales & Operations Plan. This is appropriate, provided that more things are changed than just the numbers on the master spreadsheet page. Let's assume that the latest S&OP call for the total company is projecting a 5 percent shortfall in revenue compared with the Business Plan.[1] Changing that number is easy. The hard part is to determine where the additional revenue is going to come from. Which families can be stimulated to generate increased sales? Are the resources available to support that, or if not, when will they be?

This not only calls for evaluating product families and resources. It means developing specific plans to increase sales, e.g., promotions, pricing, sales force incentives, perhaps accelerating new product launches. It means changing the Sales & Operations Plans for all families affected, then tracking performance against the new plans as the months unfold, and continuing to take corrective action as indicated.

Change the Business Plan. In the abstract, this should be easy to accept. After all, the Business Plan was put together some months before the beginning of the fiscal year. It's old. Doesn't it stand to reason that when a company is some months into the fiscal year, it will have a better handle on how things are likely to go? I think so. Well, then, why do so many companies resist changing the older plan to match the newer plan? Because as I said above, the Business Plan is a commitment to people up the line.

Do those folks up the line care deeply about whether Product Family A is 4 percent below plan and Product Family B is 5 percent above? Normally no. They're interested in the bottom line, i.e., in whether the business is going to generate the revenues called out in the Business Plan. The "mix" of revenue from family to family is normally the concern of the people running the business, as long as they deliver the bottom line.

---

[1] Back in Chapter 1, I pointed out that some publicly traded companies use two sets of numbers: one for Wall Street, containing plans expected to be attained, and one for internal purposes with stretch goals, which may or may not be completely achieved. I went on to say that they run with one set of internal numbers, the stretch goals. That point applies in the discussion that follows; the stretch plan is the Business Plan.

So I recommend that, as a general rule, the Business Plan numbers for *individual families* should be changed to reflect how the business is going to achieve the Business Plan numbers for the total business. When the sum of the individual families doesn't equal the bottom line for the total business, it's time to develop plans to cover the shortfall — and then express those plans into both the Business Plan and S&OP. And, at the end of the day, if it's not possible to hit the Business Plan, if all else has truly failed, then the bottom line of the Business Plan should be changed also.

All of the above results in running the business with one and only one set of internal numbers. People who do it that way will tell you that it's a very good way to manage.

Add New Products

During this phase, it's time to get new product introductions onto the S&OP radar screen. As we said earlier, new product launch issues need to be visible in all of the S&OP steps: Demand Planning phase, Supply Planning phase, Pre-SOP meeting, and Executive S&OP meeting. What's being worked here is the impact of new product introductions on the demand picture, the supply picture, and what problems are being created as a result of the new demand and supply issues. Where practical, the impact of new product launches should be displayed on the S&OP spreadsheets both in the quantitative section of the display and in the Comments sections.

Tie the Detail to the Summary

Sales & Operations Planning deals with volume, right? But we don't ship volume out the back door; we ship mix — individual products and orders. Mix is where the rubber meets the road.

So picture this: Company Z seems to have a great S&OP process. But their Master Scheduling operates independently and never looks at what S&OP is saying. It's disconnected. Therefore, Company Z doesn't really have a great S&OP process after all. People may be doing a lot of good work on Sales & Operations Planning, but it doesn't mean much; it's not affecting the real world.

What's needed is to add up the detail in the Master Schedules. Aggregate it into product families, summarize it by months, and compare it with the Operations Plan within S&OP. The sum of the Master Schedules for all the products within a given family should equal the Operations Plan plus or minus a few percent. I recommend that the Master Scheduler prepare a concise report, for review at each Pre-SOP meeting, showing the comparison between the S&OP numbers and the summed Master Schedules. This linkage helps to ensure that the decisions made in Sales & Operations

Planning are being transmitted downward into the detailed schedules that affect what happens in the customer order department and on the receiving dock, the plant floor, and the shipping dock.

A similar approach can be applied to the demand side. If you have forecasts for individual products, reconcile them with the aggregate Sales Forecasts in S&OP, thereby insuring that the volume plans and the mix plans are in sync.

As I said back in Chapter 4, I believe the best way to develop aggregate sales and operations plans is *not* to develop all the detail and then add it up. Rather, the detailed plans need go out only to around the Planning Time Fence, that point where the specifics of individual products must be known. For most companies, this is a matter of several days or weeks, possibly several months. What I'm recommending here is that, within that Planning Time Fence, the detail data match the aggregate. Outside of that time fence, there's little or no need for large amounts of detail.

Chapter 15

Automate Feeds into the S&OP Spreadsheets

Some companies are fortunate; they have all of the data they need for S&OP readily available and readily transportable into spreadsheets. Many have installed Enterprise Software Systems (ESS/ERP), and they're probably in good shape as far as data is concerned. If your company is in this category, you can skip this chapter and not miss much. On the other hand, if your company isn't that fortunate, you'll need to get the data you need into the spreadsheets easily and routinely.

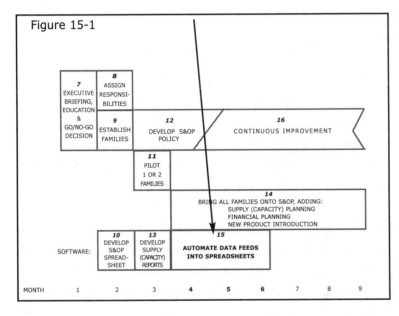

Figure 15-1

Most companies in the less fortunate category start the pilot by simply collecting and key-entering the necessary numbers directly into their spreadsheets. The reason is that frequently there will be a delay for the folks in Information Systems to automate the feeds, and so they take the line of least resistance and do the manual data entry themselves. This has the benefit of not delaying the pilot — and hence the overall implementation — and helps to get people more familiar with the spreadsheet, understand what the numbers really mean, and identify shortcomings in the data. That's fine.

However, if you stay on this path for too long, the data collection, collation and key-entry job becomes onerous as more and more families and subfamilies are added to S&OP. It's also error-prone, and it's inefficient because the folks doing the work usually don't have "data entry" in their job descriptions. They already have full-time jobs.

Therefore, it's very important that this task be taken care of early in the implementation. My advice is to start looking at this issue as soon as you decide to implement S&OP. Do you have a problem here? If so, how soon can it be taken care of? Ideally this capability would be taken care of before or during the month of the pilot so that the subsequent months can use the automated process. I've seen implementations get delayed because of this problem, and that's not good. Delays put the entire implementation at risk: no progress means decreased enthusiasm, which in turn means a greater chance that senior management will tune out. And when those folks tune out, the project will almost certainly die.

Some of you are probably thinking, "What's the big deal? This is not a terribly difficult or time consuming task. How do some companies get behind the eight ball on it?" The answer is: *priority*.

Many IS departments have large backlogs of work (owing, no doubt, to an excess of demand for their services over the supply of time they have available). The next job that comes into the department typically goes to the back of the queue, slowly works its way up the priority ladder, and — after a number of months — gets addressed and completed.

That won't work for what we're trying to do here. Manually entering increasing amounts of data into the S&OP spreadsheets can result in errors, frustration, and a slower rate of progress as more and more families are added. One of the keys in a successful implementation is to increase both the quantity and quality of the data: more families need to be added quickly, and thus the data itself must become more accurate and more complete at the same time. Key-entering data for a half dozen or more product families and perhaps several dozen subfamilies is not the way to get there.

My recommendation is, at the very onset of the project, to establish S&OP as a high-priority activity. Since this data automation step is on the critical path for implementing S&OP, then it also has high priority. Get a commitment from the IS folks to complete this step early in the project. If necessary, the S&OP Executive Champion can be called upon to help set the priorities. This task should be completed no later than a month or so following the pilot — and since it's almost never a lot of work, there's no good reason why it shouldn't be.

Chapter 16

Continuous Improvement

There are two main pieces to this important topic: internal and external. "Internal" means within the S&OP process itself, and "external" refers to processes outside of S&OP — other processes that affect customer service, inventories, customer lead times, and so forth.

Internal Improvement — Critique of the Executive S&OP Meeting

"Internal improvement" refers to improvement within Sales & Operations Planning itself. Two tools exist to help companies make continuous improvements in their S&OP processes, one of which we've already seen. It's the last item on the agenda of the Executive S&OP meeting: critique of the meeting. If you do this periodically, I can almost guarantee that you'll be delighted with how much better the meetings become. It doesn't need to take a lot of time, normally five or ten minutes.

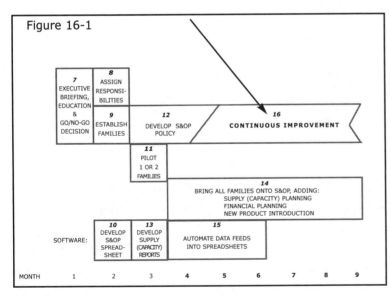

Figure 16-1

One good way to conduct this critique is to simply go around the room and ask each person to give his or her reaction to the meeting, pointing out areas for improvement. I've observed a few companies do the critique very effectively by each person's assigning a numerical grade to the meeting on a scale of 1 to 10 and stating the reason for that grade. Some companies make it a practice to let the president go last and make the concluding remarks.

However you do it, the critiques should not be viewed as bad news but rather as opportunities for improvement.

Internal Improvement — The S&OP Effectiveness Checklist

The checklist is the second element in continuously improving the S&OP process, and it is shown in full at the end of this chapter. As you can see, it contains a series of 25 items that can be answered with a "yes," a "partial," or a "no." It contains instructions for scoring the responses and evaluating how well the S&OP process is being used.

I recommend that you begin using the checklist during the month following the pilot, i.e., during month three. It's unlikely that you'll score very high on that first evaluation, but that's okay. Working the checklist at this early stage will point out the areas where you're doing well, and that's good feedback. It will also point out what remains to be done, which at this early stage, will be quite a bit. Your main focus should be on completing the items on the project schedule, so the checklist results should be viewed primarily as supporting information to the schedule. In some cases, I've seen people modify the project schedule based on results of the checklist. As you go forward into months four and beyond, the project schedule will play a diminishing role and the checklist should become more dominant in directing what needs to be done. Feel free to photocopy it.

External Improvement

S&OP's contribution to continuous improvement in other parts of the company's operations is addressed in item 12 on the checklist, which reads:

> Demand/supply strategies for each product family are formally reviewed quarterly in the Pre-SOP and S&OP meetings, with a view towards increasing customer service targets, reducing inventory targets, and reducing customer order backlog targets.

Let's say that, for one of your Make-to-Stock families, your target customer service level is 98 percent and your target finished goods level is fifteen days' supply. Let's say you've been hitting those targets for some months now. So what should be done?

What should *not* be done is to do nothing. The spirit of continuous improvement should lead the company to target either an increase in customer service, a reduction in inventory, or possibly both. So how should that be done?

Well, it's usually not enough to simply change the numbers on the page. What needs to be done is to get into the underlying processes and to start asking some questions:

• Why do we need 15 days of inventory to give 98 percent customer service?

• What process changes could we make to cut the inventory down to 12 days and not hurt customer service?

• What if we reduced the changeover time on the equipment that makes the product for this family? That means we could make shorter production runs, our inventory would go down, and customer service wouldn't drop and might even increase.

• Could we do anything to reduce the forecast error on the items in this family? If so, we'd need less safety stock and could give the same or better customer service.

• How about cutting manufacturing and purchasing lead times? If we could do that, we'd become more flexible and that means giving higher customer service with equal or lower inventories.

Another opportunity here concerns time zones and fences. Let's say that Company Y has the following time fence set at the end of month three: no production rate changes beyond +10 percent and –20 percent. When was that last changed? If it's been that way ever since they started on Sales & Operations Planning, it seems to me that they're falling down on the continuous improvement side of the process. I recommend that Operations work hard at becoming more flexible so that Company Y can give better customer service, reduce inventories, and improve its financial picture. When they become more flexible, that should be reflected in their time zones.

What I'm getting at is that there's a lot more to continuous improvement than changing the numbers on a piece of paper. Rather, the key is to improve underlying processes. The important contribution of Sales & Operations Planning here is that it raises the visibility of process improvements to the top management team and expresses them in terms that are easy for them to understand: customer service, customer lead times, and inventory investment.

THE S&OP EFFECTIVENESS CHECKLIST

COMPANY/DIVISION: _____ **DATE:** _____

1. Sales & Operations Planning is a monthly process involving both middle management and top management, including the president (general manager, COO). yes partial no

2. The monthly S&OP cycle consists of a Demand Planning phase, a Supply Planning phase, a Pre-SOP meeting, and an Executive S&OP meeting that includes the president. yes partial no

3. A written Sales & Operations Planning policy details the participants, responsibilities, timing, and objectives of each step in the process. yes partial no

4. Meeting dates for the Pre-SOP and Executive S&OP meetings are scheduled well into the future, to maximize attendance. yes partial no

5. The Executive S&OP meeting is rescheduled if the president is unable to attend. Other participants who cannot attend a given meeting are represented by their designated alternates, who are empowered to participate in the decision-making process. yes partial no

6. A written agenda is issued at least two work days before each Executive S&OP meeting, highlighting major decisions that need to be made at that meeting. yes partial no

7. The Executive S&OP meeting operates at an aggregate, family level and rarely focuses on individual items. yes partial no

8. The number of product families is in the range of 5 to 15. Subfamilies are used in the Pre-SOP steps where appropriate. yes partial no

9. Sales & Marketing "owns" the Sales Forecast. They understand and accept their responsibility: to provide forecasts that are reasoned, reasonable, reviewed at least monthly, and reflect the total demand. yes partial no

10. Operations "owns" the Operations Plan. They understand and accept their responsibility: to develop plans that support the Sales Forecast, meet the demand/supply strategies, and are cost-effective for production. yes partial no

11. Customer service performance measures (on-time and complete shipments) are reviewed at each Pre-SOP and Executive S&OP meeting. yes partial no

12. Demand/supply strategies for each product family are formally reviewed quarterly in the Pre-SOP and Executive S&OP meetings with a view towards increasing customer service targets, reducing finished goods inventory targets, and reducing customer order backlog targets. yes partial no

13. The S&OP process covers all important parts of the business and extends at least twelve months into the future. yes partial no

14. The S&OP spreadsheet contains all key information on one page: past performance to plan, customer service statistics, and future forecasts and operations plans. yes partial no

15. In addition to quantitative information, the S&OP spreadsheet also shows qualitative, verbal information in the form of assumptions and issues that need to be recognized.   yes partial no

16. To identify plant overload/underload problems, separate capacity displays are used where there is not a one-for-one match between product families and production resources.   yes partial no

17. New product development issues that may impact the demand/supply relationship are a permanent agenda item for both the Pre-SOP and Executive S&OP meetings.   yes partial no

18. The Master Production Schedule is compared, at least monthly, with the Operations Plan in S&OP to ensure that the Master Schedule is set at the levels authorized in the Executive S&OP meeting.   yes partial no

19. Sales & Operations Planning is a decision-making process. The Pre-SOP Team decides what recommendations to make to the executive group, and the Executive S&OP Team decides to accept those recommendations or adopt an alternative.   yes partial no

20. Members of the Finance & Accounting function play an important role in both the Pre-SOP phases and in the Executive S&OP meeting itself to ensure that the plans have financial validity.   yes partial no

21. In the Executive S&OP meeting, dollarized versions of the Sales & Operations Plan are compared with the Business Plan (annual budget, operating plan). As appropriate, the Business Plan is updated to reflect the new realities identified in S&OP.   yes partial no

22. In the spirit of continuous improvement, a brief critique of the Executive S&OP meeting is held before the end of each meeting. Feedback is solicited from all participants.   yes partial no

23. Minutes of the S&OP meeting detailing all decisions made are distributed within two work days after the meeting.   yes partial no

24. The Sales & Operations Planning process has become the framework for decision-making regarding all major demand/supply issues.   yes partial no

25. Improvement has been achieved in at least four of the following six performance areas: higher customer service, lower customer order backlogs, shorter customer lead times, higher turnover of the finished goods inventory, reduced unplanned overtime, lower hiring and layoff costs.   yes partial no

SCORING: YES = 1   PARTIAL = ½   NO = 0

					23 – 25: Excellent
_____	+	_____ /2	=	_____	>>> 20 – 22: Good
# YES		# PARTIAL		TOTAL SCORE	17 – 19: Fair
					less than 17: Poor

Fixing a Broken S&OP Process

What if your S&OP process is not working well? For example, people begrudge the time spent in preparation, meeting attendance is poor, teamwork is not improving, and/or the process is not productive. What should you do? To get started, I recommend you gather a small group of like-minded people, who believe in S&OP but are concerned that the current process is not working well. If possible, include someone from top management. Then proceed as follows:

1. As a group, review the **S&OP Effectiveness Checklist** on the prior two pages. This will show which individual parts of the process are not being done well and also, how you're doing overall.

2. Pay particular attention to **Checklist items 1 – 5, 12, 14, and 17 – 21**. These address top management participation, the lack of which is the number one cause of S&OP not working well.

3. If there's a problem here, go to work on fixing it. Ask yourselves, is this situation due to a lack of understanding? If so, it's almost a sure thing that insufficient or ineffective education was provided to the executive group. Rectify that. To deliver this education and to facilitate, utilize an S&OP expert, either one from within the company who has credibility and hands-on successful S&OP experience, or an outsider with the same credentials. **(See pages 80 - 81.)**

4. If top management won't agree to this, perhaps they will agree to an *assessment* by an S&OP expert, to evaluate your process and report findings to top management. If you do this, odds are that he or she will tell you much the same things that you learned from the checklist. However, the presentation of findings to top management and the subsequent dialogue can be powerful and just might result in turning things around.

5. If top management won't agree to either of these, check the **FAQ on page 85**. Do what it says, and wait for a better day.

6. If top management is engaged but the process is substandard, the checklist can help here also. Focus on **items #7 and 8** (too much detail), **item #11** (the spreadsheet and its use) and **items #19** and **#24** (decision making). Also check **pages 69 – 70**: "Tips for Effective Executive S&OP Meetings" and correct any omissions.

Here you may elect to do a "re-pilot" and then expand the process. This is often the best way to go, as the steps involved in *reimplementing* a process are much the same as in a first time implementation. If you go this route, you can use the **Implementation Plan** shown on **page 76** and **Appendix B**.

Chapter 17

Advanced Concepts

To review: Sales & Operations Planning is, among other things, a process to balance demand and supply. This monthly process culminates in the Executive S&OP meeting, where the leaders of the business make decisions regarding the demand/supply balance and ensure that the financial and operational numbers are in sync.

What follows is a series of examples of how S&OP can be used in somewhat more complex environments than a one-business, one-location operation. Please keep in mind that these examples are suggestions, based on fairly extensive experience certainly, but not "the only way to do it." For this reason, I'll make another suggestion: consider utilizing an S&OP expert to help you lay out alternatives. This can be tricky stuff, and it's important to avoid major mistakes early in the implementation. Get expert help.

Multi-Site, Multi-Business S&OP

Let's explore the issue of where executive-level S&OP decision-making should take place. Should it occur at the corporate office of a Fortune 50 conglomerate with two dozen operating businesses? How about the field sales office in Los Angeles? Or maybe the plant in North Carolina?

The answer to all of these questions is "probably not." There's a principle here: *S&OP needs to occur at that level in the organization where demand and supply come together, and where responsibility for the bottom line of the business resides.* Other parts of the overall organization can play a role; they can provide input into the S&OP process or they can review its results. For example:

- It would be difficult to "do S&OP" at the plant in North Carolina, if in fact other key parts of the business are located elsewhere, organizationally as well as geographically. Demand and supply do not "come together" at most plants. Rather, the plants are an element of the supply side of the business and one that has an important role in the Supply Planning phase of S&OP. But it's not central; it's not the pivot point for S&OP.

- Similarly, the sales office in Los Angeles could not be a focal point for S&OP. The people there may play a key role in Demand Planning, but they are not directly involved in the supply side of the business.

• The corporate office at the Fortune 50 corporation may review, directly or indirectly, the results of the S&OP processes at the individual business units. The people there might look at aggregated sales numbers, overall inventory projections, and the like. However, S&OP would not be *occurring* there. To do S&OP centrally for each of the 24 business units would result in a terribly inefficient use of corporate executive management's time, as they struggled through 24 meetings of an hour and a half each.

What's even worse, besides being inefficient, it would be ineffective. Two reasons: most people at corporate would probably lack the *intimate* knowledge of the individual businesses necessary for effective decision making, and equally important, they're not accountable for achieving the plan; accountability for that resides with the people in the business units.

Let's now look at some other examples, starting with simpler ones and moving to the more complex.

Multiple Sales/Marketing Units

When a given producing division is providing product to other business units, it needs processes to ensure that all demands are recognized. The solution often centers on determining who the immediate customers are.

Roger was the general manager of Division P. A majority of their production went to other divisions in the corporation. Roger questioned his division's ability to use S&OP effectively because they had no direct contact with the other divisions' customers. Roger said that there was no way they could do a good job of Demand Planning because they couldn't get to the customers.

His view changed when he started to look upon the other divisions as the customers. His job performance would be judged in part on how well his division was able to service these "internal customers." The better job he did, the happier his internal customers would be, and the more highly Roger's division would be regarded.

Division P's approach to Demand Planning for the sister divisions was to work closely with their people in projecting future demand, to get the best forecast numbers they possibly could. They visited these divisions once a month and were in contact with them between visits. Were the resulting forecasts "highly accurate"? Of course not. Were they better than before? Absolutely. Was there more that could be done? Yes.

The sister divisions were, in effect, distributors. As Bob Stahl, says: "Since distributor inventories mask the true demand, the forecasting process needs to look through the distributors into their customers. In this way, they will see true trends and patterns of demand." Thus, the next step for Roger's division should be to work with those Sales/Marketing units and get access to the true demand coming from their customers. (We'll have more to say about distributors and their inventories later in this chapter.)

Multiple Plants

Many companies have more than one plant, and of course S&OP has to reflect that. Naturally, companies with aligned resources have an easier time of it, and here's an example.

Company A has plants in Pennsylvania, Illinois, Texas, and California. Because Company A has aligned resources, its plants match up closely with the product families. Therefore, it was able to set up subfamilies by plant. For example, Product Family 9 is produced both in Pennsylvania and Texas, so the company established two subfamilies: Product Subfamily 9 — Pennsylvania, and Product Subfamily 9 — Texas.

These subfamilies are forecasted and planned individually in the Demand, Supply, and Pre-SOP steps. For the Executive S&OP meeting, the main focus is on the total Product Family 9. However, there are times when it's necessary to look at a subfamily, for instance when there's a serious overload in one of the plants, say Pennsylvania. Scenarios could then include:

• Transferring production from Pennsylvania to Texas, with an increase in freight costs.

• Adding a third shift in Pennsylvania, with some increase in overhead at that plant.

• Offloading some other volume from Pennsylvania to Illinois, with only a minor freight cost penalty but requiring some new equipment in Illinois, requiring a capital expenditure that is not in the current year's capital budget.

Obviously, cost is an important factor in this, and this is a good example of the importance of having folks from Finance & Accounting involved in the Supply Planning and Demand Planning phases prior to the Pre-SOP meeting.

For matrix, nonaligned arrangements, the standard Rough-Cut Capacity Planning approach works fine. Company L has an injection molding plant in Oklahoma and one in Ohio. Its forecasting needs to be done at a level of detail that allows demand to be assigned to the plants on the proper basis. In general, demand for Company L's products from east of the Mississippi River goes to the Ohio plant and the rest goes to Oklahoma.[1]

Having multiple plants usually means having remote plants, and that means that key people from each plant will need to take part in Sales & Operations Planning. Normally it's not considered practical to have these folks travel into headquarters each month for S&OP, nor — in this day of teleconferencing, video conferencing, Web conferencing and whatever — is it necessary. What can be helpful is to bring each one of these players into headquarters once during the early phases of implementation, perhaps when their respective plants are being added to the process. Some companies then bring the appropriate people into headquarters for an S&OP meeting once a year, as a refresher, and for some face to-face contact with people whom they normally don't see in person.

Global S&OP

A special problem exists for large multinational corporations, operating around the world and wanting to achieve a high degree of coordination. In other words, coordinate globally; act locally. Bob Stahl cites Percy Barnevik, the highly successful head of ABB, a large multinational, who said, "We are not a global company, but a collection of local companies with intense global coordination." Bob and I believe S&OP should support this concept.

Before we get into the nitty-gritty of this, let's review some fundamentals. S&OP balances demand and supply, and it integrates operational plans and financial plans. So, with a business operating globally, balancing demand and supply and integrating operating plans and financial plans may need to occur globally as well as locally.

The Goliath Widget Corporation[2] is one of these large multinationals doing a good job in using S&OP to achieve that intense global coordination. They believe that S&OP must provide the means to globalize where necessary and appropriate, without centralizing everything, taking away local initiative, ownership, and energy. Here's how Goliath does it:

---

[1] One way to do this, of course, is to create subfamilies by location, as we saw with Company A. An alternative is to apply historical percentages to the family forecast, for example 65 percent of the sales go to east of the Mississippi, the balance to the west. These percentages need to be periodically monitored for validity but, even with that, the net result can be less work for the folks in Sales and Marketing.

[2] A fictitious corporation, based on a number of real ones.

• The world is broken up into sections, called *entities*. An entity is defined as a geographical area where demand and supply principally align — specifically 80 percent or more of the demand is satisfied by supply sources *within the entity*. North America, Latin America, Europe, and Asia/Pacific are entities.

• The function of entities is to "localize" the S&OP process to the issues and problems unique to the area. It also helps address the cultural differences of how the people handle problems and conflict, not to mention minimizing the issues of time differences and geographical separation. In other words, it gives local ownership to the process, but at the same time it provides a defined and disciplined process to deal with global issues as they arise, through coordination among entities.

• There can be no entity if there isn't both demand and supply present within the entity. For example: India has demand but no supply, and thus it is not an entity; India's demand is supplied primarily by Asia/Pacific. Thus, India has a role in the Demand Planning phase for those entities.

• Each of the entities does the standard monthly S&OP process up through its Executive S&OP Meeting, led by a local process owner who knows the people, the culture, and the demand and supply issues.

• Please note that *inter-entity coordination* occurs in both the Demand Planning and Supply Planning phases. This is to ensure that all relevant demands are recognized and that the resources are present to meet them. In those cases where resources are insufficient due to inter-entity demand, this is addressed in the Pre-SOP step or sooner, probably including further communication and coordination among the involved entities.

• The global processes of financial review, coordination, and decision-making occur following the S&OP cycles at the entities.

Refer to Figure 17-1, which shows the monthly S&OP process expanded to include the steps necessary for global coordination.

Step 1: At Goliath, data gathering activities are done centrally. They're using a large enterprise software system (ESS/ERP), so it's one central effort to close the books at month-end and distribute the resulting data electronically.

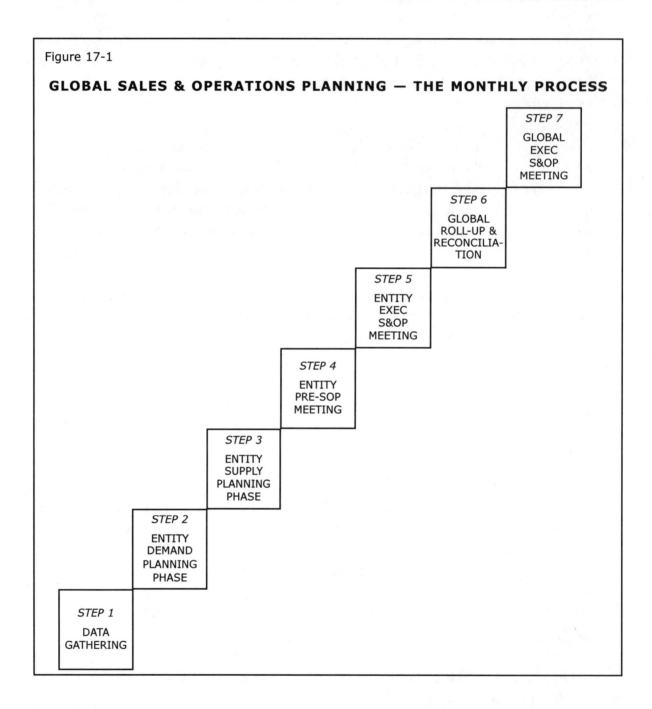

Figure 17-1

GLOBAL SALES & OPERATIONS PLANNING — THE MONTHLY PROCESS

STEP 7
GLOBAL EXEC S&OP MEETING

STEP 6
GLOBAL ROLL-UP & RECONCILIA-TION

STEP 5
ENTITY EXEC S&OP MEETING

STEP 4
ENTITY PRE-SOP MEETING

STEP 3
ENTITY SUPPLY PLANNING PHASE

STEP 2
ENTITY DEMAND PLANNING PHASE

STEP 1
DATA GATHERING

Step 2: Demand Planning is done primarily within the entities. However, sometimes portions of the markets are managed globally, meaning that some central demand people could be involved with the entities.

Step 3: Supply Planning is done primarily within the entities. Inter-entity demand is demand from one entity that is supplied from another entity, for example demand from South America supplied by North America. This is treated as a transfer of supply, with the demand showing both in the entity where it originates and the entity from which it will be supplied. Care is taken in the global roll-up phase (see step 6) not to add this demand twice.

Steps 4 and 5: The Entity Pre-SOP Meetings and Entity Executive S&OP Meetings are held within the entities in much the normal fashion. Again, one difference might be the need, on occasion, to re-communicate across entity boundaries in order to achieve a balance of demand and supply.

Steps 6 and 7: The Global Roll-Up & Reconciliation process and Global Executive S&OP Meeting are of course done centrally and attended (electronically) by key players from the entities. This is where reviews and adjustments of the rolled-up financials take place, as well as any rebalancing of global demand and supply. Rebalancing at this level occurs rarely, because it's almost always handled among the entities themselves during their S&OP cycles.

Please note: Goliath is exclusively in the widget business, and for them this model works well. On the other hand, a conglomerate — such as ABB with a portfolio of very different businesses — would use S&OP somewhat differently. The global model shown here could work nicely for each business. However, at the corporate level, the overall global process would consist almost exclusively of financial reviews, because balancing demand and supply across different businesses with widely different products is rarely a possibility.

Combination Families: Make-to-Stock/Make-to-Order, Make-to-Stock/Finish-to-Order, Etc.

Some families contain both Make-to-Order and Make-to-Stock products. Some are a mix of Finish-to-Order and Make-to-Stock. Or Finish-to-Order and Make-to-Order. In these cases, it can be useful to break out the product family into two subfamilies: say, one for the Make-to-Order products and the other for Make-to-Stock. These subfamilies are reviewed separately during the Demand, Supply, and Pre-SOP steps.

Then for the Executive S&OP meeting, combine them onto one spreadsheet for the total family. This spreadsheet might have to be a bit different. For a Make-to-Stock/Make-to-Order combination, it would almost certainly have to show both an inventory section and an order backlog section, so that these competitive variables can be visible. It may also be desirable to break out the demand separately into the Make-to-Stock and Make-to-Order components. A similar approach could be followed for Make-toStock/Finish-to-Order families.

Combination Families: Manufactured and Outsourced

Company D is in the container business. For one of its families, the product is sourced internally from one of its thirteen plants, from domestic suppliers, and from suppliers in Asia.

In this case, the product family is broken up into three subfamilies by source. The subfamilies are reviewed during the Demand, Supply, and Pre-SOP steps. The Executive S&OP meeting looks at the family spreadsheet — which in this case shows separate supply information for each of the three different sources.

Field Inventories

Company B sells through distributors, and also through manufacturers' representatives who stock the product. The inventory at these reps is on consignment; Company B owns it until it's sold. The S&OP process, to be effective, must have visibility into that inventory. Without it, a key component of the supply side of the demand/supply equation is missing. Such a lack would result in making less-effective decisions.

The inventory of Company B's products at the *distributors* is not on consignment; the distributors own it. However, shouldn't Company B be looking at the distributors' inventories of their products, even though that inventory is not owned by Company B? I certainly think so. Actually, this piece of inventory is more important than what is at the stocking reps, even though Company B doesn't own it. Why? Because it's a much bigger number; there's a lot more inventory at the distributors than at the stocking reps.

In summary, to effectively balance supply with demand, you need to see the finished inventories in the field, regardless of who owns them.

Bill Montgomery, from Orange County, California, and a leading professional in the field, points out that it's often a good practice to involve distributors and reps in the forecasting process. Here also, a Pareto approach can be used: talk to the high-volume distributors and reps. Also, it may be beneficial to talk to some lower-volume, "high-value" ones — the folks who have particular insight into the market and a good feel for what's coming down the road.

S&OP for Nonphysical Products

Company M is in the aerospace business. One of its groups makes highly engineered widgets for things that fly fast: spacecraft, satellites, and missiles, among other things. Within the Systems group, there are several separate divisions that produce and sell products. However, the *design* of the products is done centrally within the group.

Product Design and Development performs work for the producing divisions, but it also does advanced engineering projects for NASA and others. Thus, there is a wide variety of demands placed on this department. Product Design and Development also has a finite supply of engineering talent, which is not easy to increase in the short run.

Might this be a logical application for Sales & Operations Planning, even though there are no physical products involved?

Well, the group vice president had the same idea. Following successful implementations of S&OP in the product divisions, he asked the design and development folks to consider the process. They did consider it, and they adopted it, and they adapted it to their particular operation. Some of the information displayed at their meetings was a bit different, but the process itself was virtually identical to that used in the divisions that make and sell the product.

In other words, nowhere is it written that you must be making physical products in order to take advantage of this powerful tool. If you have problems balancing demand for nonphysical outputs with supply, S&OP might be a big help.

What's Coming

Let's close with a few words about the future.

On the one hand, I've learned that making predictions is a very iffy business. Some of my predictions have been amazingly accurate — right on the mark. Unfortunately, they're in a distinct minority. I might have done better with a dart board.

But it's important to think about what lies ahead, if for no other reason than to try to get ready for it. As I hope I've shown, S&OP is so helpful precisely because it is a window into the future. So here are some of my hopes (not predictions, mind you) for the continued evolution and growth of Sales & Operations Planning:

- S&OP will continue to be adopted by more and more businesses. One reason this should happen is that S&OP works, and word gets around. Another is that executives who use it become true believers in the process. As they move from one division to another or from one company to another, they take S&OP with them.

- As Supply Chain Management becomes more widely accepted, S&OP will be viewed as essential in order to balance and harmonize the entire supply chain.

- People who are experts in both S&OP and Lean Manufacturing claim that they fit together wonderfully. As the Lean movement continues to gather momentum, more of its adherents will learn and promote S&OP.

- S&OP is collaborative and cross-functional. It stands in sharp contrast to its predecessor, the process called Production Planning, which is sequential and stand-alone. As more companies become aware of the benefits of cross-functional team processes, S&OP will look increasingly attractive.

- As business becomes increasingly international, the use of Sales & Operations Planning will become "globalized" in those companies operating globally. Operating on a truly global basis can be far more challenging and S&OP can help with that, a lot.

I do hope this book proves helpful to you. Good luck and Godspeed.

Appendix A

Using the S&OP Spreadsheet
to Calculate Values
for Lean Manufacturing

By
Chris Gray
President, Gray Research
cgray@grayresearch.com
603-522-5310

Figure A-1 is an abbreviated S&OP spreadsheet showing the relationship between Sales & Operations Planning and some key concepts in Lean Manufacturing. In Chapter 4, Tom discussed *Takt Time*, *Operational Takt Time*, and *Engineered Cycle Time*. This display shows how these numbers can be derived using the S&OP spreadsheet.

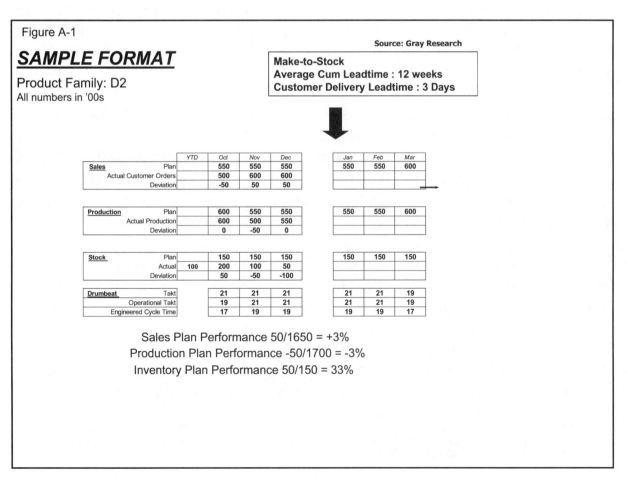

Figure A-1

In this example, Family D2 is the only product produced in its dedicated assembly cell LA002, which is the pacemaker[1] process for the production of this product family. The cell is manned 16 hours per day, five days per week, and for the sake of this example, each month is four weeks long. Obviously in the real world, there will be breaks or lunch each shift, the actual number of hours per day will be greater or less, and each week and month may have more or fewer days — all of which would be factored into the calculations. Also notice that in the example to come, all the sales, production, and inventory numbers are in hundreds of units.

Historical Data

First let's look at the historical data. Over the last three months, the Sales Plan was 55,000 per month. This means that, on average, customers were expected to require one unit every 21 seconds (16 hours per day x 3600 seconds per hour x 5 days per week x 4 weeks per month divided by 55,000). Thus, the pure Takt Time for this product over each of the past three months was projected to be 21 seconds per unit. In other words, to perfectly synchronize the plant with the marketplace, assembly cell LA002 needed to produce a finished item every 21 seconds. This is the information shown next to the Takt row of the Drumbeat section of the S&OP spreadsheet for October, November, and December.

Looking at the historical Production Plan for October, you can see the difference between pure Takt Time and Operational Takt Time. In October, the S&OP spreadsheet reflects a decision to produce 5,000 units more than required by the Sales Plan (the Production Plan is 60,000 even though the Sales Plan is only 55,000). In other words, management decided to build inventory by 5,000, which in terms of the assembly cell LA002, means that a greater volume of product must be produced in the same amount of time.

This decision is reflected in the numbers labeled Operational Takt in the Drumbeat section of the S&OP spreadsheet. The *real* Takt Time that management wanted to operate to in October was one unit every 19 seconds, or 16 hours per day x 3600 seconds per hour x 5 days per week x 4 weeks per month divided by 60,000.

(Please note: interpreting these numbers can be a bit tricky at first. When the Takt Time numbers go down, that means production volumes are going up. A Takt Time of 21 means that one item must be

---

[1] In a Lean environment, the pacemaker is that point where work is scheduled. It serves as the "drumbeat" for the entire value stream, i.e., the series of processes involved in making the product. Components produced upstream of the pacemaker are pulled to it via the pacemaker finishing schedule. Work flows to processes downstream of the pacemaker on a first-in, first-out basis.

produced every 21 seconds; a Takt Time of 19 says that you have to produce faster: one every 19 seconds.)

Once the inventory has been increased by the 5,000 units, and the Production Plan is equal to the Sales Plan, the Operational Takt Time falls back to match Takt Time. To see this, look at the November and December Operational Takt Time numbers where the Takt Time is 21 seconds and the Operational Takt Time is 21 seconds.

Of course, the Takt Time is simply a reflection of what the marketplace would like us to do, while the Operational Takt Time reflects any decisions we've made about inventory levels or other factors related to the way we want to operate our manufacturing process. As is so often the case, our desires don't automatically match our capabilities. This is where the *Engineered Cycle Time* comes in.

Engineered Cycle Time reflects what the cell is *capable of doing*. In the case of the assembly cell for D2 products, LA002, the cell design allows for an additional operator or operators to be added to the cell's team so as to reduce the cycle time per unit, and the design allows for one or more operators to be removed from the cell's team so as to increase the cycle time per unit. The manufacturing engineers responsible for LA002 have generally tried to design the cell so that it can cycle at about 90 percent of Takt Time (17 seconds when the Operational Takt Time is 19 seconds, 19 seconds when the Operational Takt Time is 21 seconds), leaving a few seconds in each takt interval for recovering from minor problems and issues in the cell.

Cell design decisions are reflected in the Engineered Cycle Time numbers for October, November, and December. In October, to support the 19-second Operational Takt Time, an additional operator or operators were to be added to the cell and the cycle time per unit was to change to 17 seconds. In November and December, at normal production volumes and an Operational Takt Time of 21 seconds, the operator(s) were to be removed from the cell and the Engineered Cycle Time adjusted to 19 seconds.

Future Expectations

What's more important for the purposes of S&OP and lean production, these Drumbeat numbers for future time periods show the relationship between what the market wants, how we would like to operate, and our capabilities — hopefully with sufficient lead time to ensure that our capabilities can be made to match demand.

For example, in Figure A1, you can see that in the future the assembly cell will be called on to operate at 21 seconds per unit through February, with increased velocity (19 seconds per unit) in each of the subsequent periods. In other words, as volume increases from 55,000 to 60,000 per month, the cell must produce faster — one finished unit every 19 seconds. Management has decided to operate the cell at the exact pace dictated by the customer — in other words, the Operational Takt Time matches the pure Takt Time. And, as we've seen in the historical numbers, the cell is designed to support it.

But what happens when demand increases? Or when a corporate decision mandates a change to the production calendar? In either of these cases, the change may be so dramatic that a significant effort may be required to redesign and rebalance the assembly cell, requiring time and resources from the manufacturing engineering staff to re-engineer the planned cycle times. By adding Drumbeat information to the S&OP spreadsheet, all the participants in the S&OP process can see clearly the work required to operate the plant at the required volumes.

A minor caveat: It's important to note that if the S&OP product families and the pacemaker processes (assembly or finishing cells) are aligned, then Takt Time and Operational Takt Time would be calculated right in the S&OP spreadsheets, for comparison against the pacemaker's Engineered Cycle Time.

However, the resources may not be highly aligned. If S&OP families are produced in several pace-maker processes, or if several S&OP families are produced in the same pacemaker, it may be necessary to calculate Takt Time and Operational Takt Time as part of Rough-Cut Capacity Planning projections for the pacemaker. Takt Time and Operational Takt Time can be calculated both for the family and for the pacemaker resource, but the comparison against Engineered Cycle Time would be done at the resource, not the family, level.

Author's note: Chris Gray has developed a set of S&OP displays based on Access and Excel, which can be used in both Lean and conventional environments. It's shareware, and thus is available at no cost; it can be viewed at grayresearch.com.

Appendix B

Sales & Operations Planning
Generalized Implementation Plan

Please note: This is a generalized plan and is meant to be tailored to the individual company plan. As such, some tasks may not be necessary and can be dropped, while other tasks may need to be added. It is designed to show the planned start and completion dates for each step and contains room for amplifying comments. Overall, this plan follows the Implementation Path diagram.

TASK	PERSON(S) RESPONSIBLE	START PLAN	START ACTUAL	COMPLETE PLAN	COMPLETE ACTUAL	COMMENTS
010 Conduct Initial Briefing						
020 Conduct Education Day						
030 Make Go/No-go Decision						
040 Determine Team Members: Demand Planning Team Supply Planning Team Pre-SOP Team Executive S&OP Team Exec Champion/Sponsor S&OP Process Owner Spreadsheet Developer Consulting Support						
050 Dates Set for Next 12 S&OP Meetings						
060 Dates Set for Next 12 Pre-SOP Meetings						
070 Product Families Identified						
080 Product Units of Measure Defined						
090 Resources Identified						
100 Capacity Units of Measure Defined						
110 Planning Horizon Set						
120 Pilot Family Selected						

TASK	PERSON(S) RESPONSIBLE	START		COMPLETE		COMMENTS
		PLAN	ACTUAL	PLAN	ACTUAL	
130 Demand/Supply Strategies Set for Pilot Family						
140 S&OP Spreadsheet Format Designed						
150 S&OP Spreadsheet Programmed						
160 First Demand Planning Process Completed						
170 First Supply Planning Process Completed						
180 First Pre-SOP Meeting Conducted						
190 First S&OP Meeting Conducted						
200 Families to Be Added in Second Set of Meetings Identified						
210 Draft of S&OP Policy Developed and Circulated						
220 Capacity Planning Display Designed						
230 Capacity Planning Display Programmed						
240 Forecast Aggregation/ Disaggregation Techniques Developed						
250 Sales and Forecast Feeds to S&OP Spreadsheet Automated						
260 Actual and Planned Production Feeds to S&OP Spreadsheet Automated						

TASK	PERSON(S) RESPONSIBLE	START PLAN	ACTUAL	COMPLETE PLAN	ACTUAL	COMMENTS
270 Actual Inventory/Backlog Feeds to S&OP Spreadsheet Automated						
280 Demand/Supply Strategies Set for All Families						
290 Second Pre-SOP Meeting Conducted						
300 Second S&OP Meeting Conducted						
310 Begin Formal Capacity Evaluation within the S&OP Process						
320 Begin to Display Financial Numbers and Tie to Business Plan						
330 Begin New Product Introduction Evaluation						
340 Begin to Tie Operations Plan to Master Production Schedule						
350 Other Significant Issues Added to S&OP Agenda: Obsolescence Special Projects Others						
360 Third Pre-SOP Meeting Conducted						
370 Third Executive S&OP Meeting Conducted						
380 Sales & Operations Planning Policy Approved by Executive S&OP Team						
390 Fourth Pre-SOP Meeting Conducted						
400 Fourth Executive S&OP Meeting Conducted						

TASK	PERSON(S) RESPONSIBLE	START		COMPLETE		COMMENTS
		PLAN	ACTUAL	PLAN	ACTUAL	
410 Formalize Business Plan Review within S&OP Meeting						
420 Evaluate Other Routinely Held Meetings for Discontinuance or Integration with Sales & Operations Planning Meetings						
430 Test the S&OP Process against S&OP Checklist						
440 All Product Families and Resources Covered by S&OP						
450 Improve and Refine the Total S&OP Process						
460 Integrate S&OP with Other Continuous Improvement Processes						

Appendix C

Resource Material

Books

Ling, Richard C. and Walter E. Goddard, *Orchestrating Success: Improve Control of the Business with Sales & Operations Planning*. New York: John Wiley & Sons, Inc., 1988.

Palmatier, George E. and Colleen Crum, *Enterprise Sales & Operations Planning*. Boca Raton, FL: Ross Publishing, 2003.

Wallace, Thomas F. and Robert A. Stahl, *Master Scheduling in the 21st Century*. Cincinnati, OH: T.F. Wallace & Company, 2003.

Wallace, Thomas F. and Robert A. Stahl, *Sales Forecasting: A New Approach*. Cincinnati, OH: T.F. Wallace & Company, 2002.

Visual Media

Wallace, Thomas F. *Sales & Operations Planning — A Visual Introduction*. Cincinnati, OH: T.F. Wallace & Company, 2003. (This is a visual CD, which contains lectures given by Tom Wallace in conjunction with the Distance Learning Center at Ohio State University. It also contains a separate file of the PowerPoint slides used in the sessions, which companies can use to help build their own internal education capabilities.)

Appendix D

Glossary

ABC Classification — The grouping of items based on their importance. "A" items are the most important; "B's" are less so; and "C" items are the least important of all. This stratification can be applied to items in inventory, products, product families, customers, and more. ABC classification is based on Pareto's Law, the 20/80 rule, which states that 20 percent of the items in a group will have 80 percent of the impact.

Abnormal Demand — Demand not in the forecast, frequently from a customer with whom the company has not been doing business.

Aggregate Forecast — See: **Volume Forecast.**

Aligned Resources — Resources that match up very closely with the product families. For example, all of the production for Family A is done in Department 1 and Department 1 makes no product for any other family; similarly for Family B and Department 2, and so on. Determining future capacity requirements for aligned resources is simpler than for matrix resources. See: **Matrix Resources.**

Assemble-to-Order — See: **Finish-to-Order.**

Available-to-Promise (ATP) — The uncommitted portion of a company's current inventory (On-Hand Balance) and future inventory, as expressed by the Master Production Schedule. ATP is an important tool in promising customer orders.

Bias — The amount of forecast error build-up over time, plus or minus. This is a measure of overforecasting or under-forecasting. See: **Sum of Deviations.**

Bill of Resources — A listing of the important resources required to produce and deliver a given product or product family. Used in Rough-Cut Capacity Planning.

Build-to-Order — Term popularized by Dell Computer; it has a similar meaning to **Finish-to-Order** and **Assemble-to-Order.** See: **Finish-to-Order.**

Business Plan — The financial plan for the business, extending out three to five fiscal years into the future. The first year of the plan is typically the annual budget and is expressed in substantial detail, the future years are less so.

Capable-to-Promise — An advanced form of **Available-to-Promise** (ATP). ATP looks at future production as specified by the master production schedule. Capable-to-Promise goes further; it also looks at what could be produced, out of available material and capacity, even though not formally scheduled. This capability is sometimes found in advanced planning systems (APS).

Capacity Planning — The process of determining how much capacity will be required to produce in the future. Capacity planning can occur at an aggregate level (see **Rough-Cut Capacity Planning**) or at a detailed level. Tools employed for the latter include the traditional **Capacity Requirements Planning** process and the newer Finite Capacity Planning/Scheduling, which not only recognize specific overloads but make recommendations for overcoming them.

Capacity Requirements Planning (CRP) — The process of determining the amount of labor and/or machine resources required to accomplish the tasks of production, and making plans to provide these resources. Open production orders as well as planned orders in the MRP system are input to CRP, which translates these orders into hours of work by work center by time period. In earlier years, the computer portion of CRP was called infinite loading, a misnomer. This technique is used primarily in complex job shops.

Collaborative Planning, Forecasting, and Replenishment (CPFR) — A process involving participants in the supply chain centering on jointly managed planning and forecasting, with the goal of achieving very high efficiencies in replenishment. CPFR has been referred to as "second generation **Efficient Consumer Response**."

Demand Management — The functions of sales forecasting, customer order entry, customer order promising, determining distribution center requirements, interplant orders, and service and supply item requirements. **Available-to-Promise** and **Abnormal Demand** control play a large role in effective Demand Management.

Demand Manager — A job function charged with coordinating the **Demand Management** process. Frequently the Demand Manager will operate the statistical forecasting system and work closely with other marketing and salespeople in the Demand Planning phase of S&OP. Other activities for the Demand Manager might include making decisions regarding **abnormal demand,** working closely with the Master Scheduler on product availability issues, and being a key player in other aspects of the monthly **Sales & Operations Planning** process. This may or may not be a full-time position.

Demand Plan — The forecast, customer orders, and other anticipated demands such as interplant, export, and samples. See: **Sales Plan.**

Demand/Supply Strategies — A statement for each product family that defines how the company "meets the customer" with that product, its objectives in terms of customer service levels, and targets for finished inventory or order backlog levels. For example, Family A is Make-to-Stock (i.e., it is shipped to customers from finished goods inventory), its target line fill is 99.5 percent, and its target finished inventory level is ten days' supply.

Demand Time Fence — That period of time in the near future inside of which the unsold forecast is ignored in the **Master Schedule.** In many companies, the Demand Time Fence is set at or near the finishing lead time for the product. The logic is that the unsold forecast can't be produced due to insufficient time and thus should be ignored. See: **Planning Time Fence.**

Design-to-Order — An order fulfillment strategy that calls for detailed design of the product to begin after receipt of the customer order. This is frequently used in companies that make complex, highly-engineered, "one-of-a-kind" products. See: **Finish-to-Order, Make-to-Order, Make-to-Stock.**

Detailed Forecast — See: **Mix Forecast.**

Distribution Requirements Planning (DRP) — A technique that employs the logic of MRP to replenish inventories at remote locations such as distribution centers, consignment inventories, customer warehouses, and so forth. The planned orders created by DRP become input to the **Master Schedule.**

Efficient Consumer Response (ECR) — An approach in which the retailer, distributor, and supplier trading partners work closely together to eliminate excess costs from the supply chain, with the goal of enhancing the efficiency of product introductions, merchandising, promotions, and replenishment.

End Item — An individual finished product.

Engineered Cycle Time — In **Lean Manufacturing**, the capacity of the resource expressed in the time required to produce one item. An engineered cycle time of 20 means that the resource is capable of producing one item every 20 seconds. See: **Takt Time.**

Enterprise Resource Planning (ERP) — An enterprise-wide set of management tools with the ability to link customers and suppliers into a complete supply chain, employing proven business processes for decision-making, and providing for high degrees of cross-functional coordination among Sales, Marketing, Manufacturing, Operations, Logistics, Purchasing, Finance, New Product Development, and Human Resources. It enables people to run their business with high levels of customer service and productivity, with simultaneously lower costs and inventories. It also provides the foundation for effective supply chain management and e-commerce. Enterprise Resource Planning is a direct outgrowth and extension of Manufacturing Resource Planning and, as such, includes all of those capabilities. ERP is more powerful than MRP II in that it: a) applies a single set of resource planning tools across the entire enterprise, b) provides real time (or near real time) integration of sales, operating, and financial data, and c) extends resource planning approaches to the extended supply chain of customers and suppliers.

EPE Interval — In **Lean Manufacturing,** this is the minimum time between production runs of each part produced in a process. (EPEI = Every Part Every Interval.) The EPEI calculation determines the maximum frequency at which each item can be run without creating problems because of the amount of set-up time required.

Executive S&OP Meeting — The culminating step in the monthly **Sales & Operations Planning** cycle. It is a decision-making meeting, attended by the president/general manager, his or her staff, and other key individuals.

Family — See: **Product Family.**

Final Assembly Schedule (FAS) — See: **Finishing Schedule.**

Financial Interface — A process of tying financial information and operating information together. It is the process by which businesses are able to operate with one and only one set of numbers, rather than using data in operational functions that differ from that used in the financial side of the business.

Financial Planning — The process of developing dollarized projections for revenues, costs, cash flow, other asset changes, and so forth.

Finish-to-Order — An order fulfillment strategy where the customer order is completed shortly after receipt. The key components used in the finishing or final assembly process are planned, and possibly stocked, based on sales forecasts. Receipt of a customer order initiates the finishing of the customized product. This strategy is useful where a large number of end products, most often due to a high degree of optionality within the product, can be finished quickly from available components. Syn: Assemble-to-Order, **Build-to-Order.**

Finishing Schedule — The schedule that defines the operations required to complete the product, from the level where its components are stocked (or Master Scheduled) to the end item level. The schedule also assigns the resources (equipment, manpower) to be utilized, and specifies timing.

Forecast — See: **Sales Forecast.**

Forecast Consumption — The process of replacing uncertain future demand (the forecast) with known future demand (primarily customer orders).

Forecast Error — The amount that the forecast deviates from actual sales. Measures of forecast error include **Mean Absolute Deviation** (MAD) and **Sum of Deviations** (SOD). See: **Variability.**

Forecast Frequency — How often the forecast is fully reviewed and updated. A monthly frequency is common.

Forecast Horizon — The amount of time into the future that the forecast covers.

Forecast Interval — The size or "width" of the time period being forecasted. The most commonly used intervals are weekly or monthly.

Heijunka — A Japanese word that means "balancing." A Heijunka mechanism in **Lean Manufacturing** balances the amount of workload with the capacity to do it, normally in very small time increments. It also typically involves sequencing orders in a repetitive pattern.

Independent Demand — Demand for an item is considered independent when unrelated to the demand for other items. Demand for finished goods and service parts are examples of independent demand.

Just-in-Time — The forerunner of **Lean Manufacturing.**

Kanban — A method used in **Lean Manufacturing** in which consuming (downstream) operations pull from feeding (upstream) operations. Feeding operations are authorized to produce only after receiving a Kanban card (or other trigger) from the consuming operation. In Japanese, loosely translated it means card or signal. Syn: demand pull.

Lean Manufacturing — A powerful approach to production that emphasizes the minimization of the amount of all the resources (including time) used in the various activities of the enterprise. It involves identifying and eliminating non-value-adding activities in design, production, **Supply Chain Management,** and customer relations.

Load Profile — See: **Bill of Resources.**

Line Fill Rate — The percentage of order lines shipped on time and complete. See: **Order Fill Rate.**

Make-to-Order — An order fulfillment strategy where the product is made after receipt of a customer's order. The final product is usually a combination of standard items and items custom designed to meet the requirements called out in the customer order. See: **Design-to-Order, Finish-to-Order, Make-to-Stock.**

Make-to-Stock — An order fulfillment strategy where products are finished before receipt of customer orders. Customer orders are typically filled from existing finished goods inventory. See: **Design-to-Order, Finish-to-Order, Make-to-Order.**

Manufacturing Resource Planning (MRP II) — See: **Enterprise Resource Planning.**

Master Schedule — The tool that balances demand and supply at the product level, as opposed to **Sales & Operations Planning,** which balances demand and supply at the aggregated **Product Family** level. It is the source of customer order promising, via its **Available-to-Promise** capability, and contains the anticipated build schedule for the plant(s) in the form of the **Master Production Schedule.**

Material Requirements Planning (MRP) — The first step in the evolution of ERP. This set of techniques uses bills of material, inventory data, and the **Master Production Schedule** to calculate requirements for materials. It makes recommendations to release replenishment orders. Further, since it is time phased, it makes recommendations to reschedule open orders when due dates and need dates are not in phase. Originally seen as merely a better way to order inventory, today it is thought of primarily as a priority planning technique (i.e., a method for establishing and maintaining valid due dates on orders). See: **Manufacturing Resource Planning, Enterprise Resource Planning.**

Matrix Resources — Resources that do not match up with the product families. For example, Department 1 makes products in Families A, C, D, and G. Determining future capacity requirements for matrix resources is somewhat more complex than for aligned resources. See: **Aligned Resources.**

Mix — The details. Individual products, customer orders, pieces of equipment, as opposed to aggregate groupings. See: **Volume.**

Mix Forecast — A forecast by individual products. Sometimes called the detailed forecast. It is used for short-term scheduling for plants and suppliers (and may be required for certain long lead time, unique purchased items).

On-Hand Balance — The amount physically in stock, irrespective of booked customer orders.

Operational Takt Time – See: **Takt Time.**

Operations Plan — The agreed-upon rates and volumes of production or procurement to support the **Sales Plan (Demand Plan, Sales Forecast)** and to reach the inventory or order backlog targets. The Operations Plan, upon authorization at the **Executive S&OP meeting,** becomes the "marching orders" for the Master Scheduler, who must set the **Master Production Schedule** in congruence with the Operations Plan. Syn: **Production Plan.**

Order Fill Rate — The percentage of customer orders shipped on time and complete as opposed to the total number of orders. Order fill is a more stringent measure of customer delivery performance than line fill. For example, if only one item out of twenty on a customer order is unavailable, then that order counts for zero in the order fill calculation. The line fill percentage in this example would be 95 percent. See: **Line Fill Rate.**

Pacemaker — The point at which work is scheduled in a **Lean Manufacturing** environment. Components produced upstream of the pacemaker are pulled to the pacemaker finishing schedule. Work flows to processes downstream of the pacemaker on a first-in first-out basis.

Planning Bill of Material — An artificial grouping of items in a bill-of-material format used to facilitate forecasting and Master Scheduling.

Planning Time Fence (PTF) — The period of time inside of which detailed planning must be present in the **Master Schedule.** Normally, the Planning Time Fence approximates the cumulative lead time of the product plus 25 to 50 percent. Sometimes called the Critical Time Fence. Most Master Scheduling software will not alter the **Master Production Schedule** within the PTF, only outside of it.

Plant Scheduling — The process of creating the detailed schedules needed by the plant(s). Plant schedules can include the **Finishing Schedules,** fabrication schedules, and so forth.

Postponement — An approach that calls for waiting to add options into the product until after the customer order is received and then finishing the product very quickly. See: **Finish-to-Order.**

Pre-SOP Meeting — The preliminary session prior to the **Executive S&OP meeting.** In it, key people from Sales & Marketing, Operations, Finance, and New Product Development come together to develop the recommendations to be made at the Executive S&OP session.

Product Family — The basic planning element for **Sales & Operations Planning.** S&OP's focus is on families and subfamilies (volume), not individual items (mix).

Product Subfamily — A planning element sometimes used in S&OP that provides a more detailed view than product families, but not at the extreme detail of individual products. Product Family A, for example, might contain three subfamilies — A1, A2, A3 — and each of those might contain a dozen or so individual products. See: **Product Family.**

Production Plan — See: **Operations Plan.**

Projected Available Balance — The inventory balance projected out into the future. It is the running sum of on-hand inventory, minus requirements, plus scheduled receipts and (usually) planned orders.

Pull — The process of flowing production from upstream (feeder) processes to downstream (finishing) processes in which nothing is produced by the feeder until the downstream "customer" signals a need.

Resource — Those things that add value to products in their production and/or delivery.

Resource Planning — A generalized term applied to **Manufacturing Resource Planning, Business Resource Planning,** and **Enterprise Resource Planning.**

Resource Requirements Planning — See: **Rough-Cut Capacity Planning.**

Rough-Cut Capacity Planning — The process by which the **Operations Plan** or the **Master Production Schedule** can be converted into future capacity requirements. Frequently the Operations Plan, expressed in units of product, is "translated" into standard hours of workload (which is a common unit of measure for production operations). Rough-Cut Capacity Planning can be used at the departmental level, or for subsets of departments, down to individual pieces of equipment or specific skill levels for production associates. This process can also be carried out for suppliers, for warehouse space, and for non-production operations such as product design and drafting.

Rough-Cut Material Planning — The generation of future requirements for materials via calculating Rough-Cut Material Requirements from the **Master Schedule** for short- to medium-term requirements and from the **Operations Plan** for longer-term needs, thus bypassing **Material Requirements Planning.** This process is very similar to **Rough-Cut Capacity Planning.**

Safety Stock — An amount of inventory held to protect against fluctuations in demand and/or supply.

Safety Time — A technique in MRP whereby material is planned to arrive ahead of the requirement date. This difference between the requirement date and the planned in-stock date is safety time.

Sales & Operations Planning (S&OP) — A business process that helps companies keep demand and supply in balance. It does that by focusing on aggregate volumes — product families and groups — so that mix issues — individual products and customer orders — can be handled more readily. It occurs on a monthly cycle and displays information in both units and dollars. S&OP is cross-functional, involving General Management, Sales, Operations, Finance, and Product Development. It occurs at multiple levels within the company, up to and including the executive in charge of the business unit, (e.g., division president, business unit general manager, or CEO of a smaller corporation). S&OP links the company's Strategic Plans and **Business Plan** to its detailed processes — the order entry, **Master Scheduling, Plant Scheduling,** and purchasing tools it uses to run the business on a week-to-week, day-to-day, and hour-to-hour basis. Used properly, S&OP enables the company's managers to view the business holistically and provides them with a window into the future.

Sales Forecast — A projection of estimated future demand.

Sales Plan — The details backing up the **Sales Forecast.** It represents Sales & Marketing management's commitment to take all reasonable steps necessary to achieve the forecasted level of actual customer orders.

Stockkeeping Unit (SKU) — An individual finished product. In the more rigorous use of the term, it refers to a specific, individual product in a given location. Thus, product #1234 at the Los Angeles warehouse is a different SKU from the same product at the Chicago warehouse.

Subfamily — See: **Product Subfamily.**

Supermarket — Within **Lean Manufacturing,** this is a set amount of inventory (finished goods or work-in-process) that allows **Pull** processes to function when demand is not totally linear.

Supplier Scheduling — A purchasing approach that provides suppliers with schedules rather than individual hard copy purchase orders. Normally a supplier scheduling system will include a contract and a daily or weekly schedule for each participating supplier extending for some time into the future. Syn: vendor scheduling.

Supply Chain — The organizations and processes involved from the initial raw materials through manufacturing and distribution to the ultimate acquisition of the finished product by the end consumer.

Supply Chain Management — The planning, organizing, and controlling of supply chain activities.

Supply Planning — The function of setting planned rates of production (both in-house and outsourced) to satisfy the **Demand Plan** and to meet inventory and order backlog targets. Frequently, **Rough-Cut Capacity Planning** is used to support this.

Takt Time — In **Lean Manufacturing,** Takt Time sets the basic rate of production. It communicates the frequency of demand and thus the frequency at which products must be produced at the **Pacemaker. Takt Time** is derived from the Sales Plan, while **Operational Takt Time** is derived from the Operations Plan, reflecting inventory draw down or build up, plant shutdowns, and other factors. Thus, these values can be thought of as the *demand* for capacity, i.e., what the resource will be required to produce. **Engineered Cycle Time** refers to the *supply* of capacity, i.e., what the resource is capable of producing.

Time Fence — A point in the future that delineates one time zone from another. See: **Time Zones.**

Time Phasing — The process of expressing future demand and supply by time period.

Time Zones — Periods within which changes are managed in certain ways, reflecting the realities of the operating environment. For example, in many plants, achieving a 30 percent increase in output might be impossible within three days; difficult and costly, but attainable, within three months; and very practical within three years.

Two-Level Master Scheduling — A Master Scheduling approach where an end product type or category (not a specific product) is Master Scheduled along with selected key options, features, attachments, and common parts.

Variability — In the larger sense, this is the amount that individual elements in a time series deviate from the average. In some cases, variability is random and inherent in the process being observed. See: **Forecast Error.**

Vendor Managed Inventories — A process that places the replenishment decision-making in the hands of the supplier. It's the supplier's job to ensure that the customer does not run out of stock and to keep the inventories at the agreed-upon levels.

Volume — The big picture. Sales and production rates for aggregate groupings — product families, production departments, etc. — as opposed to individual products, customer orders, and work centers. See: **Mix.**

Volume Forecast — A forecast by product groupings such as families, classes, and so forth. Also called the aggregate forecast or the product group forecast, it is used for sales planning, for **Capacity Planning** at the plants and suppliers, and for financial analyses and projections.

Appendix E

The Difference between Production Planning and Sales & Operations Planning

Perhaps the best way to contrast Sales & Operations Planning with its predecessor, Production Planning, is to view them graphically. On the next page, please see Figure E-1, showing the Production Planning method.

Notice that the Sales Planning and Production Planning boxes are separate and sequential. What's implied by this is that Sales & Marketing puts together a forecast and hands it off to Operations, who puts together a production plan which is sent directly into Master Production Scheduling.

Figure E-2, depicting Sales & Operations Planning, looks quite different. It shows both the sales planning function and the operations planning function occurring jointly, not sequentially. It indicates that there is interaction between the Sales Plan and Operations Plan, which of course is what I've been presenting throughout this book.

The result of the cross-functional Sales & Operations Planning process is the companywide game plan for Sales & Marketing, Operations, Finance, and Product Development — far more than a production plan.

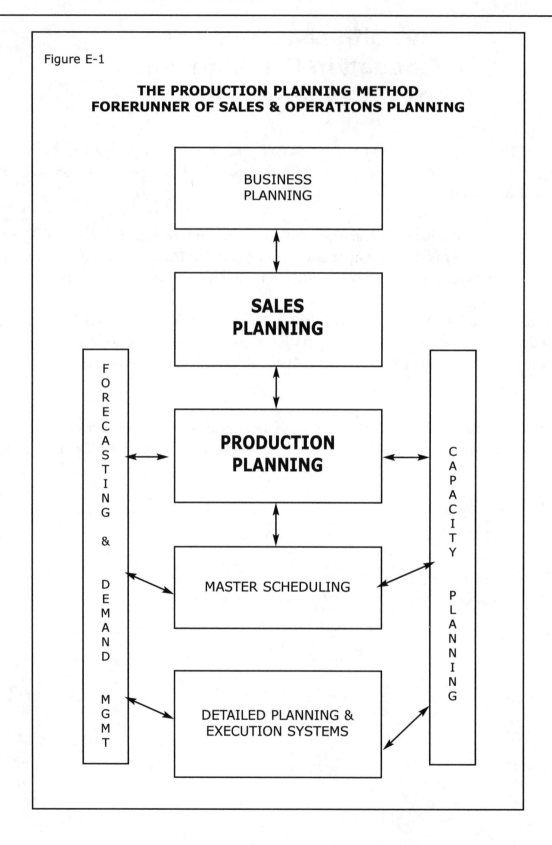

Figure E-1

THE PRODUCTION PLANNING METHOD
FORERUNNER OF SALES & OPERATIONS PLANNING

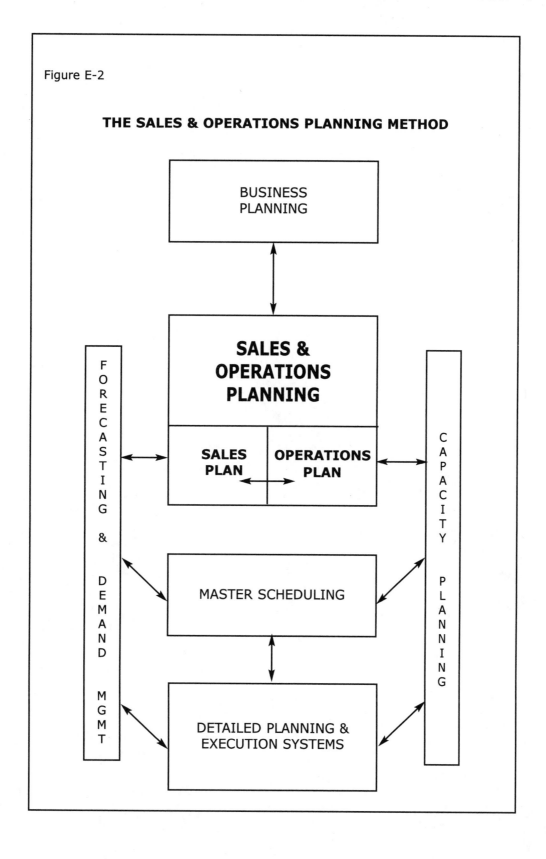

Figure E-2

THE SALES & OPERATIONS PLANNING METHOD

Appendix F

Nontraditional Uses of Rough-Cut Capacity Planning in Conjunction with S&OP

Please refer back to the Bill of Resources in Figure 4-3 and note that there are two non-production resources shown: Warehouse Space and Supplier A. Let's look first at the supplier issue.

Rough-Cut Material Planning

It's possible to use Rough-Cut Capacity Planning for suppliers. It's called Rough-Cut *Material* Planning, and it can be used to project future purchased material requirements more easily, and perhaps more validly, than the conventional method.

What is the conventional method? Well, many companies will extend their item-level sales forecasts and Master Schedule far out into the future. Then they'll use Material Requirements Planning (MRP) to explode material requirements from the Master Schedule, which they'll then pass on to key suppliers. Even some companies heavily into Lean Manufacturing will do this, despite having "turned off" MRP for order releasing and instead use a Kanban, demand-pull method.

Using Rough-Cut Material Planning with S&OP makes it possible to bypass MRP, and to send to the suppliers aggregate projections of volume many months into the future. In almost all cases, the suppliers don't care whether they'll be making 1000 gallons of formula B1 and 3000 of formula B2 six months from now, or whether it'll be 3000 gallons of A1 and 1000 of B2. In most cases, the suppliers need volume estimates upon which to plan their capacity; they normally don't need specific mix information until closer in.

What is important is that they'll need to have the resources to produce about 4000 gallons of this product and ship it to the customer. In those cases where it would be helpful for the supplier to know the mix between A1 and B2, the Bill of Resources could contain the two formulas and show the demands separately.

In terms of how the information is displayed for the suppliers, it tends to be simpler than the displays we saw for internal resources. A common approach is simply to list the aggregate requirements by month, and let the suppliers relate those numbers to their demonstrated capacity. Often, the suppliers will be producing for a number of customers, and thus comparing one customer's requirements to capacity that's serving many customers is not an apples-to-apples comparison, and hence can be misleading.

In summary, Rough-Cut Material Planning requires less work and often results in information that is more valid than can be had using the conventional, detailed approach.

Warehouse Space Planning

Now let's take a look at the warehouse opportunity. If we know the average cubic feet (or perhaps square feet or number of pallets) per product family, then we can multiply those numbers by the planned inventory balances for the families and thus derive the amount of warehouse space each family will require. Next, we can combine the space requirements for each family into an overall warehouse space requirement for the business. This could be particularly helpful for seasonal businesses, as shown in Figure F-1.

<u>Figure F-1</u>

WAREHOUSE SPACE PLANNING

DEMAND FOR WAREHOUSE SPACE (in 000 square feet)

Family	A	M	J	J	A	S	O	N	D	J	F	M
A	50	50	50	50	50	50	50	50	50	50	50	50
B	10	10	10	10	10	10	10	10	10	10	10	10
C	0	20	40	60	80	60	40	20	0	0	0	0
Required Space	60	80	100	120	140	120	100	80	60	60	60	60

SUPPLY OF WAREHOUSE SPACE (in 000 square feet)

	A	M	J	J	A	S	O	N	D	J	F	M
Available Space	90	90	90	90	90	90	90	90	90	90	90	90
Space short			10	30	50	30	10					

In Figure F-1, Product Family A is sold to retailers who require the company to maintain certain levels of finished goods inventory. Family B contains the company's proprietary products and much of Lean Manufacturing has taken hold there. (There is a minimal level of finished goods expected in order to allow for nonlinear demand.) Family C is highly seasonal, with the pre-build beginning in May but the selling season not starting until September.

This information states that additional space will be required during August through November, and how much. Given a good S&OP process and reasonably valid load factors (square feet per product), the Logistics people can make arrangements for outside warehousing with confidence that the amounts shown here are definitely "in the ballpark" as to how much space will be needed. That's because these numbers are drawn directly from the Sales Forecast and Operations Plan approved by top management in the Executive S&OP meeting.

Index